LIFE IS A GIFT

LIFE IS A GIFT

A practical guide to making
your dreams come true

GILL EDWARDS

piatkus

PIATKUS

First published in Great Britain in 2007 by Piatkus Books Ltd
Reprinted 2009

A CIP catalogue record for this book
is available from the British Library

ISBN 978-0-7499-2781-3

Text design by Briony Hartley
Edited by Liz Dean

Data manipulation by Action Publishing Technology Ltd, Gloucester
Printed and bound in Great Britain by
CPI Mackays, Chatham, Kent

Papers used by Piatkus are natural, renewable and recyclable
products sourced from well-managed forests and certified
in accordance with the rules of the Forest Stewardship Council.

Piatkus
An imprint of
Little, Brown Book Group
100 Victoria Embankment
London EC4Y 0DY

An Hachette UK Company
www.hachette.co.uk

www.piatkus.co.uk

For my son Kieran.
May you always remember who you are –
and reach for your wildest dreams

Contents

Acknowledgements

My infinite love and gratitude to Abraham (and Esther and Jerry Hicks), whose teachings have so enriched my understanding of inner-outer reality, and whose wise and loving words fill my heart and soul daily. My thanks also to Seth (and Jane Roberts), whose books first blew my mind 25 years ago, and whose footsteps helped me to find my own path – and to Orin (and Sanaya Roman), Lazaris (and Jach Pursel), Emmanuel (and Pat Rodegast) and many others who have brought wisdom from the higher dimensions; to earthly pioneers of the new metaphysics such as Louise Hay and Shakti Gawain; and to the many shamanic teachers who have helped to keep my spirituality grounded, embodied and connected to Mother Earth.

My gratitude to all the mystics, dreamers and visionaries who have been willing to be heretics, to be guided by their inner Light and refuse to follow the crowd – including those scientists, doctors, healers, channels, therapists and spiritual teachers who are birthing a new paradigm into the world. Thank you for your courage, your passion, your wisdom – and for lighting the way.

Thanks to my wonderful publishers for their ongoing support and positive approach over so many years – with particular thanks to Gill Bailey and Helen Stanton.

Thanks to Liz Dean for her editorial comments; and, as always, to my parents for their careful proof-reading and helpful suggestions.

My warm thanks to friends and clients who have held up mirrors for me, and pushed me to love and to grow; thank you for being who you are. My eternal love and gratitude to my *anam cara* – the man who taught me what unconditional love really means; thank you for your presence and your absence, and for all the precious pearls. And, as always, my deep love and gratitude to my family and close friends for being there for me, and sharing the journey along the smooth and rocky paths. Thank you for being such amazing gifts in my life.

Foreword

Love is life believing in itself.
Manitongquat[1]

If you have a dream, you *can* make it come true. No matter what has happened in the past. No matter what your starting point. No matter what anyone else thinks. That much is guaranteed. You only have to understand the laws of reality creation – then get out of your own way, so that the Universe can deliver its gifts.

Does this make it sound simple and straightforward? Well, it is and it isn't. After 25 years of study and 17 years of writing and teaching about *how* we create our reality, I'm still learning. I still trip myself up and make messes. I still make detours from the smooth path I had intended. But this is an essential part of the journey. Whenever you stub your toe, it wakes you up. Unless you get lost in rage at the uneven path, or in beating yourself up for being clumsy, every challenge makes you look within. It makes you ask some bigger questions. And it always yields precious pearls. Each time, I pick myself up, dust myself off and continue along the path – hopefully a little wiser, more compassionate and more loving, and always with a clearer vision of what I want to create. Which releases even bigger dreams for the future. Every day feels precious and wonderful to me, and I've made some truly magnificent dreams come true in my own life – as well as making a positive difference to many thousands of other lives.

I grew up in a haunted house, which awakened me to unseen realities from an early age. It also gave me an insatiable curiosity about the nature of life, and our relationship with the unseen realms. As a teenager, I read countless books about mysticism and the paranormal, studied Freud and Jung and learnt yoga and meditation. I began to ask some Big Questions about life, and my spiritual journey began in earnest. Many years on, after working as a clinical psychologist throughout the 1980s and as a spiritual author and workshop facilitator ever since, that curiosity about life is as sharp as ever. But I now have some amazing answers to my Big Questions about life – along with practical tools for transformation – that restore the joy, passion and magic to everyday living and provide positive, empowering approaches to our personal and global issues.

Three things I've come to know for sure: Firstly, life is a gift. It is not a lesson, task or mission. We are not here to be good or perfect. We do not have to prove ourselves worthy. (We *are* good. We *are* worthy.) We are not here to sort ourselves out; nor are we here to rescue the world. We are here for a joyful adventure in consciousness on this beautiful planet we call Earth. Secondly, everything that happens is governed by the law of attraction. There are no victims. The outer world is a mirror of our inner world of thoughts, beliefs, desires, fears and expectations. Thirdly, this is a loving cosmos. There is a creative and loving higher force – whom we might call God, All That Is, Source or the Universe – who loves us unconditionally, says yes to *every* heartfelt desire we have, and guides us constantly towards fulfilment of those desires.

We are apprentice gods and goddesses, capable of turning lead into gold and water into wine. If only we could keep fear, doubt, insecurity, regrets, duty, guilt, blame and judgment out of the way, we could create miracles. If only we could stay focussed upon what we desire. If only…! As a psychotherapist, I have witnessed how readily people get in their own way – usually following family-ar habits of thinking and behaving that were set up in childhood. Habits that can become invisible, even as they trip us up. Habits we stoutly defend and justify, even as they make us miserable. As I know from personal experience, keeping out of our own way is our greatest challenge.

Awakening to love

Like many others, I believe we are living in an age of awakening. Our old ways-of-seeing no longer seem to be working. Chaos and disorder seems to be a necessary precursor to transformation, and many people are going through rapid and often unexpected changes – as if we are being *forced* to change, personally and globally. A new holistic world view is emerging from science and mysticism, and creeping into every corner of society. A cultural revolution is underway.[2] Once mostly behind the scenes, it is now becoming more and more public and obvious.

Humanity is shifting into a new state of awareness, which can leave us confused and uncertain at times, as if we are walking upon shifting sands. We are moving beyond the limiting old world of fear, struggle, lack and victimhood – the 'common sense' world which we have inhabited for centuries – and stepping into a bright new realm of love, freedom, joy, creativity and awareness. We are shifting from fear into love. We are evolving from caterpillars into butterflies. But how hard we sometimes cling to our 'safe' and familiar old world. Afraid of spinning our cocoon. Afraid of letting go. Afraid of being alone. Afraid to trust in our own process. Afraid to believe in our dreams. Afraid to open our wings, and fly.

The positive side of this emerging world view is that nothing and no one 'out there' has to change so that you can be happy. Happiness is always created from the inside out. The down side is that there is no one to blame any more. Whatever happens, the finger always points towards you. And the danger is that you might beat yourself up for 'creating' illness, accidents, redundancy, a burglary, lawsuit or painful relationship – which keeps you in a downward spiral of shame and self-sabotage. This book will remind you that challenges are merely opportunities to love, grow and set yourself free – and are always leading you, however indirectly, towards where you want to go.

Once you see life as a gift, you can relax and breathe more easily. You have nothing to prove. There is nothing wrong with you. There is nothing wrong with anyone else. It is impossible to make a mistake, or to do anything wrong. Even when life looks messy, you are doing just fine. But the caterpillar must spin a dark cocoon before it can metamorphose into a butterfly. Despite the many challenges we are facing, everything is unfolding perfectly. We are evolving into a new state of awareness, and a new understanding of love.

Love is the energy that connects – that allows us to reach out, to connect with others, to break free from our old defences, to expand and grow, to see the bigger picture. Love allows us to become more of who we are. As you love yourself, others and the world without condition – as you make peace with what is, while reaching towards what you desire – you can create your own heaven on earth.

The good news is that you can forget about struggle and efforting. Taking a nap is often more helpful! If it seems like hard work, or you feel trapped or stuck, you are not aligned with the creative forces of the cosmos. When you are going with the flow, any action feels joyful and liberating. Freeing up your resistance, so that you can ride the flow of energy that underlies the visible realm, is the key to making your dreams come true. If it feels great, if it makes you smile, if it helps you breathe more easily, you are moving in the right direction. If it feels heavy, painful or difficult, you are going against the flow. (And in a loving Universe, doesn't that make sense?)

Making your dreams come true

Life is a Gift is a practical guide to creating your own heaven on earth. This isn't a superficial cookbook for 'getting more toys' – although you *can* have anything you want. It is about learning to flow with the Universe. It is about becoming a divine co-creator, a practical mystic, a passionate dream-weaver. It is the meeting point of your spirituality, your creativity and your sensuality. It is the journey of the embodied soul – the creator, lover and visionary. It is about becoming a spiritual adult, and stepping into your birthright as a human being. It is about forging a deeper connection with your higher self, and creating a life that truly belongs to you. Above all, it is a book about unconditional love.

This slim volume holds the mystical secrets of the Universe. You could read this book in a couple of hours, but putting it all into practice will take a lifetime (or more) to master. And what fun you can have along the way! I suggest that you have a notebook and pen handy. Plenty of soul-searching, inner reflection and creative fun lies ahead. And lots of miracles. Once you really *know* – deep down in your belly – that you create everything that happens to you, that you are deeply loved and the Universe is always on your side, life becomes a truly magical journey.

By the time you have finished this book, you will know the steps involved in creating joy, inner peace and fulfilment, and making all your dreams come true – and you will have a practical toolbox for life. In turn, the chapters reveal:

✧ Why life needs to be seen as a loving gift – rather than a task, mission or accident

✧ The mystical law that governs *everything* that happens to us

✧ Understanding emotions as your primary form of higher guidance

✧ How to listen to the inner voice of love (rather than fear)

✧ How to direct your thoughts like laser beams

✧ Why struggle is a waste of time, and why to follow your bliss

✧ How everything is always unfolding perfectly, personally and globally

✧ How to make a positive difference in the world

✧ Why to live for today, while dreaming about tomorrow

Life is a Gift shows you how to stay connected to the unseen flow of the Universe – which is the secret to creating your own heaven on earth. You will soon know, moment by moment, whether you are moving towards or away from your dreams and desires; and what to do if you have wandered off your path. And as you put these tools into practice, miracles will begin to unfold.

Gill Edwards, April 2007

Chapter One

Life is a Gift

The basis of life is freedom. The purpose of life is joy.
The outcome of life is growth. **Abraham**[3]

Last night, I dreamt I was a deer – roaming free through the forest, leaping over bracken and streams, pausing to graze in a woodland clearing, my ears twitching and alert, my eyes and nose alive to all around me. Then I awoke from my dream, rose from my bed and opened the wooden shutters. Morning light poured into the room, and I gazed into the garden. A few paces away, beneath an oak tree, a roe deer looked up and gazed at me. For a split moment, I felt my ears twitch – and did not know whether I was deer or human.

In the Native American tradition, the deer is a symbol of gentleness and unconditional love. It reminds us that love is the great healer, which overcomes the illusion of separation. When love is present, there is no fear. When there is no fear, everything is welcomed into your heart – and you relax deeply. Love reassures us that all is well. It sets us free. Love is all about reaching out, embracing and integrating. Love unites and connects us, whereas fear disconnects. Darkness is merely the absence of light – and, like the morning light, love pours in unless we are shutting it out.

Our creation myths

How would you answer the two eternal questions of life: *Who am I? And why am I here?* Such questions might seem airy-fairy and irrelevant to everyday life. You might even be wondering when we will get to the practical tools for making your dreams come true. (That starts in the next chapter.) But first, we need to explore your philosophy of life.

Your cosmology has a profound impact on your daily life – whether or not you have ever seriously considered it. Your answers to the eternal questions reveal your creation myth and this, in turn, affects almost every choice you make. Your creation myth is the foundation stone of your personal relationships, and your mental and physical health. It determines whether you create a wonderful and fulfilling life, or whether you feel trapped or driven, or secretly think there must be more to life than this. Your cosmology even drives decisions such as whether to eat that slice of chocolate gâteau, whether you work through your lunch break, or whether you allow yourself to dance barefoot in the rain.

As a child, you will have worked out answers to the eternal questions, whether consciously or not, largely by observing how your parents (and others) went about their lives: What their priorities were. How they spent their time. How they behaved towards each other. How they treated you. How they dealt with emotions. How they handled problems or conflict. How they made decisions. What they saw as the good and right thing to do. And the messages you received about God, life and the cosmos from your family, friends, school, religion and the culture around you. Almost every sentence we utter, and every action we take, reveals something about our cosmology. As an adult, those old beliefs tend to lurk around in your subconscious – and unless you reconsider and make new choices, they can make a huge difference to how you think about your life. And as we shall see, how you think about yourself and your life is *everything*.

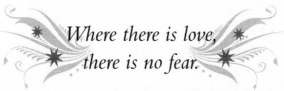

Where there is love, there is no fear.

As I see it, there are three basic creation myths, which can be roughly ascribed to religion, science and embodied mysticism. You don't have to make a decision about which creation myth to choose right now – but you do need to be aware of these different ways of seeing reality, and how they shape and control you. Otherwise the ideas in the chapters that follow might sit uneasily with you, without your knowing why.

MYTH ONE: LIFE IS A TRIAL
Most of the world's religions (and much New Age philosophy) promote the idea that life is a trial, test, challenge or
mission – that the earth is a training school for wayward
souls, and the purpose of life is to 'perfect' yourself. You
are here to learn lessons. You are here to prove yourself
good and worthy. The underlying message is that there
is something wrong with you (or the world) that needs
to be fixed, that you are inadequate, that you must seek
redemption or fulfil an unknown task or mission. And if
you succeed, you will get your reward in the afterlife (or
at least burn off bad karma). This creation myth implies
that the earth is a fallen place, a vale of tears – and that
God and heaven are elsewhere, a long way away. You are
exiled from the promised land. It often places a stern
father-figure in the sky wagging a judgmental finger over
you – awarding gold stars every time you are good in His
eyes, and totting up black marks for each 'sinful' thought
or deed. Or giving you brownie points for hard work,
suffering and self-sacrifice. And it urges you to guide your
life by ancient and dusty texts, or by the social norms, or
by meeting others' needs and expectations – rather than
being guided from within.

This cosmology is based upon judgment, or *conditional*
love. It is judgment – splitting the world into good and
bad, or right and wrong – that destroys our inner peace,
and is the source of every war, feud and ongoing conflict
on the planet. Yet it has been encouraged for thousands

of years by religions that urge us to 'be good' – on the assumption that, unless our impulses and desires are kept under control, we would be immoral and destructive. Deep down, we are seen as inherently bad. And the problem is that defining *any* part of ourselves (or others) as bad or wrong throws us into conflict. When you see life as a battle between good and evil – a battle that you might win or lose, day after day – you have to keep on your toes, and make sure you are being good enough. And make sure others are being good, too. And watch over your shoulder for the bad ones!

When a child is told that Santa Claus will only visit if they have been 'good', or finds out they will be punished if they are 'bad', they are learning this harsh creation myth. *'Be good! Do as you are told! Please others! Put your own feelings and needs aside. Then you will be rewarded.'* Jam tomorrow. Or the next day. Or after you die. In the meantime, your reward might be approval from others, worldly success, or a warm glow of righteousness. But the price you pay is that you are being moulded and controlled by others. When you are taught to be good, you are not learning to be true to yourself, or to love yourself. If anything bad happens, you see yourself as being punished – or being tested. You learn to suppress your own emotions and desires, in the vain hope of earning or deserving love. Your priority is being good and perfect in the eyes of others. You are guided from outside yourself, and learn to conform. You hide behind roles, and do what is expected. You jump through hoops to please others. You develop an inner judge or critic who keeps you (and others) in check. It becomes hard to relax.

You live in fear and insecurity – constantly treading on eggshells – since you are taught that love is conditional. Conditional upon being good and perfect. Conditional upon being whom others want you to be. Which is not love at all. It is merely approval.

Love is what remains when you release fear and judgment.

MYTH TWO: LIFE IS AN ACCIDENT

A more recent creation myth emerged from science in the seventeenth century, when science was officially separated from religion.[4] This myth suggests that life on earth is a random, statistical accident. An accident so unlikely as to be quite miraculous – but an accident nevertheless. In Western society, this is the myth that is widely agreed to be 'common sense', so we all carry this myth within us too. According to this myth, we are isolated beings hurtling through space on an inert lump of rock, in a mostly dark and empty universe. Only the solid stuff that you can see and touch is real. Life starts with conception, and death is the end. The existence of God, angels and the unseen realms is seen as unnecessary and irrelevant, or even dismissed as childish fantasy.

On the positive side, this scientific myth disposes of the judgmental god who throws down thunderbolts when displeased. On the negative side, it sees us as the hapless victims of luck, chance and coincidence. It sees life as unpredictable and chaotic. Accidents can happen. Disaster might hit you. Illness might strike you down. You never know what is around the next corner. It suggests that we can only control our lives by actively controlling our circumstances, and safeguarding ourselves against threats, danger and potential enemies.

If you believe in this myth, your priority is staying safe and secure. You might become afraid of taking risks. Afraid of change, afraid of letting go. Or you might become controlling towards others. It is a myth that promotes beliefs in lack, scarcity and competition. After all, in a solid reality, there is only so much to go around. *If you have more, I have less. We are gobbling up the earth's limited resources.* It urges you to seek security 'out there' – perhaps through money, pensions, insurance, status, material possessions or needy relationships.

This is a creation myth based upon fear and separation. As we shall see, it means that we try to change or control life from the outside in, instead of from the inside out – which leads us into pain, struggle and self-sabotage. Psychologically, this myth leaves us feeling anxious and vulnerable, or lonely and empty. Within this mythology, life has no inherent meaning or purpose. It is mundane and ordinary. There is no spark of magic. Happiness often feels precarious, as if the rug might be pulled from under you at any time. And love is nowhere to be found.

MYTH THREE: LIFE IS A GIFT
Since ancient times, there has been an earth-centred cosmology, still held by many tribal cultures, which sees us as inseparable from God and nature. In Western society, this ancient way was hunted down, outlawed and forced underground for many centuries. But in recent decades it

has emerged from the increasingly popular mystical side of the world's religions, and (perhaps more surprisingly) from the cutting edge of modern science.[5] According to this creation myth, everything that exists was birthed from the body of God. Instead of seeing us as isolated beings, this myth sees creation as an undivided whole. It sees all of creation as good and divine – since everything is part of God. And it suggests that life is a wondrous gift from this loving, conscious and ever-evolving Source.

You are a creative spark of divine energy.

This ancient/new cosmology gives life a far more positive agenda. When you see life as a gift, the earth becomes a playground. From this holistic viewpoint, we are all creative sparks of divine energy. You are inseparable from God/Source, and that same creative force is flowing through you. You are loved. You have nothing to prove. Your goodness and worthiness are never in question. You are an eternal being of Light – and the purpose of life is joy. You are here to enjoy this adventure-in-consciousness that we call life. Look at that glorious rainbow, the sunbeams gleaming on the lake, the mist hanging in the valley, the woodland rich with bluebells, or the child splashing in the puddle! Taste the sweet dripping flesh of a peach. Feel the soft warm skin of your lover. Listen to that crackling log fire, or the autumn leaves crunching beneath your feet. The Universe delights in your pleasure. It revels in your joy and laughter. It glorifies in your sensuality and sexuality. It relishes giving and receiving love. And it adores your creativity and individuality and desires – which help the world (and God) to grow and evolve. Growth is inevitable – but our *purpose* is joy.

When your cosmology reflects a Universe based upon unconditional love, it is a powerful tool for liberation. It restores a connection to your own divinity. It sweeps away the old cobwebs of fear, guilt, judgment and control. It beckons you through a sunlit gateway into a new world – an expansive world of love, light and joy. A world of freedom. When you see life as a gift, you know this is a planet of free will. This means there are no right or wrong choices. (The life-is-a-trial myth, by contrast, will warn you that you do have free will, but you must make the *right* choice. The choice that God wants you to make. Or else.) In a Universe based upon love, our freedom comes with no conditions. We are free to choose and, as we shall see, the Universe supports our decisions and preferences. In every case. Without reservation.

As metaphysical writer Neale Donald Walsch puts it, what God wants is – nothing.[6] Nothing at all. No needs, no demands, no expectations. No hidden agendas. No duties or responsibilities. There is no judgment, so you can do nothing wrong. There are no risks, and mistakes are impossible. Life is forever unfolding, and you can always make fresh choices as you go along. This is a world of unconditional love. Once you see life as a gift, you can relax. Your priorities are joy and delight, love and freedom, adventure and creative self-expression. Instead of holding back from life, inhibiting yourself, suppressing your desires or denying your feelings, you can jump in with both feet – as exuberantly alive as a puppy, rolling and tumbling across the grass.

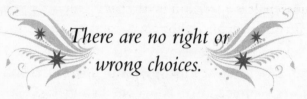

There are no right or wrong choices.

I believe that great spiritual teachers such as Jesus and Buddha all taught unconditional love and oneness – before their teachings were distorted by political agendas, mistranslation and misunderstanding.[7] If you believe in goodness and badness, it splits you in two. You live in a world of duality. William Blake rightly said that the only sin was the accusation of sin. The mystical poet Rumi, likewise, said that when we go beyond ideas of wrong-doing and rightdoing, our soul can lie down in the grass.[8] We become embodied souls. We become enlightened.

Unconditional love has the power to transport us into a new world. To make us fully alive. To make us whole. Instead of splitting heaven and earth apart, a cosmology of unconditional love knits them back together. Instead of original sin, it offers original blessing.[9] This is a creation myth that releases our potential, which allows miracles to burst forth.

Embodied mysticism honours much that has been denied or denigrated for centuries: our emotions, our intuition, our dreams and visions, our body, our sensuality, our sexuality, our passion, our desire, our inner wisdom and power, our sense of mystery and wonder. It restores an earthy and embodied spirituality. It reclaims what we have split off and lost. It might be seen as the awakening goddess – the return of the divine feminine – the immanent god who is interwoven through all things, seen and unseen. It is a creation myth that is empowering, positive, affirming, joyful, celebratory – and, above all, loving.

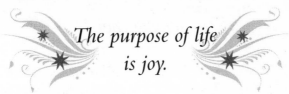

The purpose of life is joy.

Love versus fear

These three creation myths give us three strikingly different guidelines for our lives:

✧ Be good *(Life is a trial)*

✧ Stay safe *(Life is an accident)*

✧ Be happy *(Life is a gift)*

You don't have to be a clinical psychologist like me to figure out which of these mythologies promotes happiness and mental health, and which undermine it. Any cosmology that promotes fear or judgment should carry a serious health warning. It is guaranteed to make you anxious, guilt-ridden and neurotic – and often ill. It gives you a battle mentality.

Believing there is something wrong with you – that you have to earn or deserve love, and prove your worthiness – makes you vulnerable to depression and despair.

It means you forever live in fear of getting it wrong. It means you strive to be good and perfect in the eyes of others, instead of expressing who you really are. You try to justify your existence, rather than simply enjoying life. It makes you vulnerable to addictions such as workaholism, exercise or compulsive shopping. You feel unlovable or inadequate, and try to cover up what feels bad or unacceptable. Or – even more dangerous – you project your imagined 'badness' onto other people, then battle against those you see as bad, wrong or dangerous. Not only are you on trial, so is everyone around you. (In a recent snippet I overheard from the spoof TV series *The Simpsons*, a character comments that she's just spent a week at Bible camp 'learning to be more judgmental', which gave me a wry smile.) If you view life as a trial, it becomes more important to be good and virtuous than to be happy. You become more concerned about how your life *looks* from the outside than with how it *feels* from the inside.

Seeing life as a trial makes inner peace and joy almost impossible. Yet our cultural heritage means that we all carry this cosmology within us. It has been passed down the generations as a method of social control, and our collective consciousness is drenched in it. Likewise, taking the modern secular view – seeing life as a random accident, with no inherent meaning or purpose – is not designed to make you deliriously happy! Threats hang over you in both cosmologies. The threat of bad luck, tragedy, disaster, disapproval, rejection, abandonment – even the threat of eternal damnation.

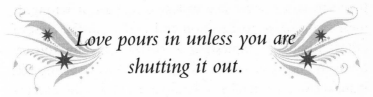

Love pours in unless you are shutting it out.

Spirituality for grown-ups

These three cosmologies seem to mirror our natural evolutionary process, from child to adolescent to adult. As I see it, humanity has been passing through the child-like dependency of seeing life as a trial – and seeking love and approval – for the past three or four millennia. Then we made a brief stay in the adolescence of seeing life as an accident – with its denial of the existence (or relevance) of God. And we are now moving into a mature and liberating cosmology in which we see ourselves as co-creators with a loving Source who works *with* us to help us create our own heaven on earth. This requires us to be fully responsible for our lives. It also requires us to love without condition. This is spirituality for grown-ups.

I'm biased towards seeing life as a gift, since I believe it can transform our lives and our world. I see the fear-based cosmologies as rather like cancer cells – weak, sick cells that can attack their own host. We all have cancerous cells within our body, but most of the time, these cells are scooped up by the immune system as unhealthy and thrown out. But if you attack yourself repeatedly through guilt and insecurity, or feeling trapped, power-less and afraid, or pleasing others at your own expense, or secretly blaming and resenting others, or dwelling on what is bad or wrong or dangerous, or just seeing life as empty and pointless – if you eat away at yourself – the self-attacking cancer cells are strengthened, and your self-loving immune system is weakened. The sick cancer cells can then gang up together and take charge of your life. But the real cancer is your cosmology – your toxic beliefs about life, God and the cosmos.

Nothing is more central to your life than whether your creation myth is based upon love or fear. It makes the difference between feeling separated from love, or feeling connected. It makes the difference between fulfilling your dreams and desires, or settling for what is expected. It makes the difference between feeling safe in the world, or feeling under threat. It makes the difference between loving and intimate relationships, or relationships based upon conformity, control and self-sacrifice. It makes the difference between feeling anxious, guilty and depressed, or joyful, relaxed and open-hearted. A cosmology based upon love means that you can find inner peace, which means you can build peaceful and loving relationships. Then we can all build a peaceful and loving world.

> *Love unites and connects us.*
> *It makes us whole.*

The wound of separation

Once you see life as a gift, you can take a deep breath. Ah, the sweet relief! Life does have a purpose. You are here to enjoy yourself! You are here to revel in the beauty of the earth, the joy and sensuality of being physical, the fulfilment of creativity. You are here to love, to laugh, to connect deeply with others. There is nothing wrong with you other than the belief that there is something wrong with you (or with others, or with life). Your only wound – the wound that we all share – is the belief in separation. Separation from a loving God. Separation from each other. Separation from nature. Separation from who we really are. And it is love that reconnects us. Not the conditional love of a mythical god who requires you to be good or perfect, but unconditional love. Love that cherishes every part of you. Love that honours and affirms who you are. Love that allows your energy to flow freely. Love that restores your connection to your creative Source.

Seeing life as a gift changes everything. The cosmos is seen as purposeful, intelligent and loving. In place of a cold, hard, tame, dry and dusty cosmology of the head that sucks life out of you, you discover a warm, juicy, wild and succulent spirituality of the heart, which breathes life into you. You begin to feel safe and loved in the world. These creation myths can drive your thoughts, feelings and behaviour in almost opposite directions, since they offer dramatically different perspectives on life. If you hold a creation myth based on fear and judgment, your path through life is going to be a rocky one. If your cosmology is based on unconditional love, you can and will create your own heaven on earth. In other words, your creation myth determines whether you live in mundane black and white, or in dazzling technicolour.

According to the emerging cosmology I am about to reveal, you can have, do or be anything that you want.

Does this sound wildly romantic or idealistic? I do hope so. I believe that life is meant to be heaven on earth. And yes, I do know what is going on in the trouble spots of the world, the ecological threats to our planet, and the vast array of global challenges we face. As a psychotherapist, I know about the widespread abuse that happens behind closed doors, and the private unhappiness and despair that is often concealed by public smiling faces. Yet most of this misery can be traced back to our unhealthy creation myths – from seeing ourselves as separate from Love, from living in a world of duality. A mystical world view assures you that Love is here and now – and is always reaching out towards you.

> *Heaven is a state of consciousness. It is feeling your connection to Love.*

Which brings me back to my dream about the deer. Our new understanding of reality suggests that the inner and outer realms – that is, mind and matter – are intertwined in quite magical ways. We are shifting into a staggering new perspective on reality in which we are not merely passive observers, not scientists peering down a microscope, but active co-creators of our world. There is no real separation between inner and outer reality. From a dualistic world view based on fear and separation, the deer appearing in my garden as I awoke from my dream was a mere coincidence. From the life-is-a-gift perspective, it was a synchronicity – a meaningful coincidence that comes from the ever-present interweaving of inner and outer. It reminds us that life is far more magical than it seems. That we live in a loving Universe. That heaven can be here and now.

Seeing life as a gift is not only likely to make you happier and healthier; as we shall see in the following chapters, there are good reasons to suppose that the cosmos is deliberately designed to give us whatever we ask for – to offer us an endless abundance of gifts. No strings attached. In other words, unconditional love is built into the very fabric of the Universe. Making your dreams come true is not about pulling rabbits out of hats. It is not just a clever bag of tricks. It is about moving towards a healthy creation myth. It is about allowing the natural energy of the Universe to flow through you. It is about choosing awareness and love and expansion. Then you can become a butterfly – and create the life of your dreams.

Just for you

CIRCLE OF DREAMS

Draw a huge circle on a large sheet of paper. Inside the circle, write down everything that you wish to have, do or be – perhaps within the next two or three years. What is your ideal life-style? Craft yourself a new life. Let yourself be a dreamer and visionary. Think big! Let it feel wonderful as you pour your dreams on to the clean white sheet. Know that this is the first step in reality creation. You are asking the Universe to deliver gifts to you. And the Universe always says yes. Nothing and no one stands in your way except you. Creating your own heaven on earth is entirely in your hands – or rather, in your consciousness.

Alternatively, you might want to write down qualities that you wish to invite into your life – such as love, joy, beauty, sensuality, romance, adventure, imagination, freedom, opportunity, laughter, community, teamwork, opening, creativity, nature, spirituality.

(For the past 15 years, I've drawn my own Circle of Dreams on every solstice and equinox, which are powerful times for manifesting. It is fascinating to look back and see how my dreams come into reality, often in unexpected ways.)

QUESTIONS FOR THE UNIVERSE

What are your big questions about life? What do you long to understand more deeply? What inner conflicts are you trying to resolve? What do you feel is missing in your life? What might be blocking you from your dreams? What do you need higher guidance about? Find a special notebook or journal, and write down your questions. These are questions for the Universe, Source, God/Goddess or Infinite Intelligence. Trust that your questions will be answered. You might be given books or ideas or conversations that give you fresh insights. You might be sent people, events or experiences that lead you towards the answers. You might receive your answers in times of quiet reflection and stillness. Look back at your questions in a month or a year from now, and you will be amazed at how the cosmos has replied.

Chapter Two

The Wondrous Secret

*Each person experiences a unique reality, different from
any other individual's. This reality springs outward
from the inner landscape of thoughts, feelings,
expectations and beliefs. Seth*[10]

Since ancient times, a mystical secret has been passed
down the generations – mostly by word of mouth, often
in hushed tones of secrecy and protection, and only to
those deemed ready to receive it: the initiates, chosen
ones or magical apprentices. This wisdom was considered unsuitable for the ears of the general public – even
dangerous – and has been hidden and suppressed until
now. It is only in recent decades that this secret has been
released, like singing birds from wicker cages, from the

far corners of the earth. It has come from mystics and shamans in tribal cultures. It has emerged from the cutting edge of science, especially physics and biology. It has been whispered in the age-old esoteric and mystery traditions. And it is a common thread in modern channelled teachings about the true nature of reality. It is an idea whose time has come.

The wondrous secret is heretical, and threatens conformity and social control. That's why it has been kept secret for so long. It can make mavericks of us all. It releases our limitless power and potential. It bestows the ability to change our lives forever – and make our wildest dreams come true.

Perhaps you grew up believing that much of life 'just happens' – that we can be victims of accidents, or illness, or betrayal, or violence, or tragedy, or plain bad luck. You might see yourself as ruled by fate or destiny or karma. Or you might have been told that God is in charge – so whatever happens, you must like it or lump it. You might even have been warned against having hopes and dreams for the future, so that you would avoid the pain of disappointment or heartbreak. But once you understand the mystical secret of the Universe, you never have to feel like a victim again. You will no longer give your power away to anyone or anything outside you, since you will know that you are a creative spark of the divine – an apprentice god or goddess – and that your true power lies within.

So what is the wondrous secret? It is the only law that is truly universal – to which there is no exception. No escape clause. No small print. It is based upon an awareness that, as the new physics has discovered, the world is not a solid place. What we perceive as physical reality is, in fact, a vast field of interconnected *energy*. This conscious, infinite web of energy might be called Source, God, All That Is or the Universe (with a capital U). In other words, our separateness is an illusion. We are inseparable from everything else, since we are cells in the energetic body of God.

> *Our separateness is an illusion.*
> *Everything is interconnected.*

Once you see the world as energy, you realise we are not so much solid beings of flesh and bone as we are psycho-energetic, or vibrational beings. There is no real distinction between mind and matter, since energy is all there is – whether it is visible energy like a chair or candlestick, or invisible energy like a thought or radio wave. Physics tells us that at least 90 per cent of the universe is an unknown, invisible form of matter-energy known as dark matter; that is, 90 per cent of the universe is a complete mystery to us. Could this refer to the unseen dimensions, the hidden tapestry of the cosmos, which mystics have often spoken about? This might sound very abstract, but it has huge practical implications for our everyday lives. Which brings us to the great secret.

The world as a mirror

The wondrous secret is known as the law of attraction: that is, like attracts like. As modern physics suggests, it is *consciousness* that determines what happens at a quantum level – and so, in turn, what unfolds in physical reality. Thoughts are patterned energy which pull strings in the hidden tapestry of the cosmos. Energy dances to the tune played by consciousness – and *you* are the piper who is playing the tune. You are dreaming your own world into being. Your thoughts become reality. British astronomer James Jeans said that the Universe is more like a great thought than a great machine – which is the giant shift in perspective that we are currently making. The world beneath our feet is no longer as solid as it once seemed.

The law of attraction reveals how mind and matter are interwoven in our everyday lives – and allows us to step into a magical reality in which we can have, do or be anything that we desire. We walk upon our own dreams, or nightmares, or somewhere in between. There are no limitations other than those we believe in.

In case your eyes are already glancing skywards, dismissing this as the bizarre rantings of a mad woman living in la-la land, let me reassure you that some of the most eminent people in history understood the law of attraction – such as Plato, Socrates, Shakespeare, Newton, Blake, Da Vinci, Beethoven, Thoreau, Emerson, Goethe, Einstein. You can find it hidden in the mystical teachings of every religion from Christianity to Hinduism, from Islam to Buddhism; and in ancient civilisations such as Egypt and Babylon. Countless spiritual teachers now affirm the law of attraction. And more and more leading-edge scientists agree that mind is built into the very fabric of matter – that consciousness seems to mould and even create physical reality.[11] So if I *am* crazy, at least I am in excellent company. (Phew!) Even if it sounds crazy to you right now, come along for the ride – and see whether it begins to make sense. I believe I am only reminding you of what you already know, though you might have forgotten it for now.

So how does the law of attraction work? In simple terms, our thoughts, desires and intentions are vibrational patterns of information to which the world around us resonates. Whatever you hold in your mind is emitted like a radio signal into the cosmos. Then the Universe sends events, circumstances and relationships that match that signal. In other words, your outer world mirrors your inner world. There is no reward or punishment involved in this. The law of attraction is non-judgmental; you simply get what you focus upon.

The outer world mirrors your inner world.

Keep thinking the same old thoughts, and you keep attracting the same old reality. This is why the rich tend to get richer, while the poor get poorer. If you focus on and expect prosperity, you attract it. If you focus on debt and bills, you attract more of the same. If you focus on feeling lonely and longing for a partner, you attract more loneliness and longing. If you focus on loving yourself and others, you attract loving relationships. If you focus on illness and disease, then no sooner will you cure one symptom than another one appears. If you focus on health and well-being, and assume your body is healthy and strong, then you attract good health. If you focus on mere survival and getting through the days, life will feel like drudgery and routine. If you focus on joy and creativity and love, life will be enriching and meaningful. If you focus on feeling trapped or imprisoned, you attract people and circumstances that reinforce that. If you focus on feeling free and unlimited – or just set that as a clear intention – you attract relationships and situations that support that feeling. Even the news reports you hear, or stories that others 'happen' to tell you, or conversations you overhear in a café, mirror some aspect of your own thoughts, beliefs, desires, fears and expectations.

Thoughts become things

Nothing happens at random. Even the tiniest event is governed by the law of attraction. There is no luck or chance or coincidence. The inner and outer realms are connected at a deep invisible level, and the outer reality of everyday life is simply a manifestation of our inner world. This is a looking-glass world, in which our private thoughts are manifested in physical reality. This does not happen immediately, since we have the helpful buffer of time in which to change our minds. But over time, thoughts become things. Thoughts with high vibrations – positive, joyful and loving thoughts – attract what you desire. Thoughts with low vibrations – based on fear, doubt or judgment – block whatever you desire. Whatever happens is giving you feedback about the radio signals you are sending out. And once you understand this, you can consciously create your own reality.

You get what you focus upon.

When I was a child, I dreamt of being a writer. I wanted to write books that made a difference, books that transformed people's lives. Night after night, I would fall asleep imagining bookshelves lined with books I had written, meeting with my publishers, or sitting at my desk in a large country house, poring over a manuscript. Many years later – after writing dozens of magazine articles, and working as a clinical psychologist for a decade – my dream became a reality. I live in a fairytale house beside a lake and waterfalls, nestling in the mountains amidst a stunning national park, and have written books that have changed countless lives. Dreams can and do come true – if you use the law of attraction.

Let us imagine, just for now, that life is a dream and you are the dreamer. What kind of dream would you wish to create? Set your imagination free. Where would you live? Who would you live with? How would you spend your time? How would you feel? If you could do, be or have anything at all, what would you choose? What did *you* dream for the future when you were a child? What are your dreams now?

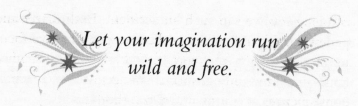

Let your imagination run wild and free.

'Oh yes', you might say, 'but get real! Someone like me can't expect the lifestyle of my *dreams*. You don't understand the limitations I have to put up with: my health, my finances, my education, my partner, my family, my boss, the small-minded town I live in. You don't understand my duties and responsibilities, and the pressures I'm under from other people. You don't know about the burdens from childhood I'm carrying, and the poor choices I've made in the past.'

But that is the magic of the wondrous secret. Nothing that has happened in the past, no current situation or circumstances, no other person or system or government, *nothing* can block you from making your dreams come true. Only you. You are your only obstacle. You cannot use anyone else as an excuse. No one can 'do' anything to you. You create everything that happens to you, even when common sense (from our solid-world perspective) suggests that it is someone else's doing.

An amusing report on motor insurance claims once quoted a driver as saying, 'The pedestrian I knocked over admitted it was his fault, as he had been knocked down last month.' This is not such a joke once you understand the law of attraction. The more the pedestrian blamed himself for the first accident, and the more he ruminated on it, the more likely it was to happen again. Then he attracted another driver who resonated with the idea of being involved in such an accident. Both driver and pedestrian felt like victims – but we get what we focus upon, and what we expect. In other words, insurance companies are only insuring us against the practical consequences of our own negative thoughts.

'But I had an accident last year,' you might protest, 'and I wasn't expecting *that*.' Yet you will have harboured thoughts and emotions, probably over a long period, which matched up with having an accident. Perhaps you needed time off work, and didn't know how else to create it. Perhaps you kept telling yourself you were a bad driver, or that you had been lucky never to have a crash. If you recall your emotions in *response* to the crash – perhaps anger, irritation, frustration, guilt, despair, depression or helplessness – those emotions will have been lurking around for a while, and the eventual *outcome* of that negativity was an accident (or illness, or lawsuit, or whatever). There are no accidents. Every event is orchestrated – in minute detail – by the law of attraction.

Let me add a note here about blame and responsibility. The law of attraction is not a reason to *blame* yourself for every negative event – which will simply attract more of the same. It is a fascinating opportunity to reclaim your power, and become a conscious creator of your own life. This is the crucial difference between blame (which disempowers) and responsibility (which empowers). Blame carries judgment.

continued ...

> Blame and guilt make you curl up in a painful ball,
> and come from seeing life as a trial; whereas respon-
> sibility gives you response-ability, and comes from
> seeing life as a gift. If it feels bad, you have tilted
> towards blame instead of responsibility.
>
> *You are never to blame,*
> *but you are always*
> *responsible.*

If you grew up with parents who routinely thought in negative ways, saw life as a struggle, blamed others for their pain, complained and criticised, put themselves down, viewed awful circumstances or relationships as 'crosses they had to bear', expected the worst, saw themselves as good and others as bad, avoided 'rocking the boat', worried about money or their health (or about you), or behaved like victims or martyrs, then those self-destructive ways of thinking and behaving might have become habitual for you too. That old way of seeing the world will feel family-ar, or just 'how things are' – and the Universe will jump through hoops proving that you are right! What is more, you will attract friends, colleagues and even casual acquaintances who share your negativity, and confirm that your fears and doubts and complaints are justified. You might feel trapped and imprisoned. You might know deep down that life is not meant to be like this. But you quietly resign yourself to a life that falls far short of your dreams.

The good news is that it is never too late to change. Perhaps you are deeply in debt. Perhaps you have a dire medical diagnosis. Perhaps you believe that your childhood left you hopelessly scarred. Perhaps you regret some of your choices, or think you took a wrong turning somewhere along the way. None of that matters. You can always create the life that you want *from where you are*. That is how this magical and loving Universe is set up. It is how the amazing gift of life is designed.

But you will need to make changes. You might need to create more time for silence, stillness and reflection – time to centre yourself and listen to your inner wisdom. You will need to deliberately choose new thoughts, and question your old beliefs. You might need to make peace with where you are, in order to open the door to change. You will also need to make new choices on a daily basis – based upon knowing that life is a gift, that you are good and worthy, and that all your desires can be fulfilled. And you will need to trust your inner guidance. Then the Universe can lead you towards a new life. The life you have been waiting for.

> *The present moment is always your point of power.*

You are never a victim of your past. The present moment is always your point of power. If you change your thinking, you change your reality. You immediately begin to attract new circumstances and events, new friends and relationships, new opportunities, new ideas and possibilities towards you. It does take deliberate effort and focussed awareness – after all, it is much easier to carry on thinking the same old thoughts – but within a few days or weeks, you could begin to turn your life around. Fresh thoughts, fresh future. And you can start to *feel* better within hours or even minutes.

It is estimated that we have 60,000 thoughts per day. If you were to focus just 51 per cent of these thoughts on the positive – what you desire, what you enjoy, what you appreciate, what is good in others, what is good in you, happy memories, happy daydreams and fantasies and joyful expectations for the future – you will s-l-o-w-l-y attract more of what you desire. You move beyond the tipping point, and your life will begin to change for the better. If you reach for 75 per cent positive thoughts, you will feel fantastic – and miracles will flow in. When your desires, beliefs and expectations are in synch, you are invincible!

Changing life from the inside out

You don't have to believe this. You can test it out. Choose new and positive thoughts about any subject, such as your job, relationships, health or money, and hold those new thoughts consistently for just 21 days – or simply don't cancel your new thoughts with any opposing thoughts – and see how the Universe responds with new situations, fresh opportunities, unexpected gifts and meaningful coincidences. It is miraculous. Or observe someone else's life, and see how it matches what they repeatedly talk about, or how they see the world. Do they talk of their dreams and visions, and all that is good and wonderful in life? Or do they speak about their problems, what is wrong with the world, what is wrong with others or their own inadequacies?

Your outer world always matches the radio signals you are emitting. And it's no use putting on a brave smile, and *pretending* to be happy and positive, or mouthing affirmations which you do not believe, since the Universe responds to your energy – to the pattern and frequency of your vibrations – not to your outward appearance or false words. You cannot fool the cosmos. You can only change your life from the inside out.

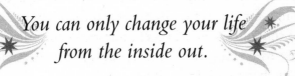

You can only change your life from the inside out.

Manifesting is not about controlling or manipulating. In fact, trying to control people or events is an act of self-sabotage, since it comes from lack of trust and faith. Controlling means trying to change your life without changing your vibrations – trying to change life (or other people) from the outside in. This leads to struggle, efforting, poor timing and damaged relationships, and rarely brings any lasting rewards. Manifesting is much more about surrender than about control. It is about letting go. It is about aligning with the natural forces of a loving Universe – putting forth your desires and preferences, then getting out of your own way.

Unfortunately most of us have countless years of practice in getting *in* our own way! We have been steeped in a 'blame culture', which supports the idea that, if things are going wrong, it must be someone's fault. Either there is *something wrong* with me, or there is *something wrong* with you, or *something wrong* with the world – and if only you could get rid of that badness or limitation, all would be well. But the very idea that there is 'something bad or wrong' keeps you trapped in the problem, instead of moving towards the solution. It keeps you stuck in a battle mentality – seeing life as a trial – which only strengthens the opposition. Whatever you push against simply pushes back at you, since we get what we focus on. The harder you push, the stronger it gets. (The war against cancer. The war against terrorism. The war against poverty.) You can have whatever you want, as long as you do not send out contradictory thoughts. Battle thoughts. You simply need to be a powerful laser beam that states: 'This is my desire'. Full stop.

Whatever you resist persists.

Sabotaging yourself

Most of us are like flickering candles rather than laser beams, cancelling out our desires almost as soon as we think them. You might say, 'I would like this – but here is why I cannot have it, or should not expect it, or do not deserve it, or might not *really* want it, or how other people or past decisions are blocking me from having it, or what is wrong with the world that prevents it, or why it is so painful for me not to have it, or what has caused me to feel so stuck, or why I should be grateful for what I have instead of wanting anything else, or why I am justified in wanting this even though others might disagree, or why I might eventually be able to have it, but will have to wait or struggle for a long time first...' You think 'If only...' or 'Yes, but...' thoughts: 'If only I had more money...' 'If only I didn't have these commitments...' 'If only my partner or boss was more supportive...' 'Yes, but my childhood was so dysfunctional...' 'Yes, but I'm not talented enough, or clever enough, or rich enough...' (Can you hear that martyred sigh?) The Universe says yes to your desire, then it hears all your wittering about why you cannot have it – and since it can only mirror back what you are giving out, it patiently keeps your gift on hold until you send out clear and consistent signals.

Some of the most common forms of self-sabotage are:

✧ Focussing on what is bad or wrong or missing right now

✧ Criticising, complaining or judging others

✧ Blaming someone else (even silently) for your own pain, stuckness or frustration

✧ Focussing on what others are doing 'wrong', or why you are 'in the right' (and getting others to support you)

❖ Explaining, defending or justifying *why* things are as they are

❖ Analysing what is 'wrong' with you, or what you are doing wrong

❖ Blaming the past, or having regrets

❖ Blaming or criticising yourself *('It's all my fault!', 'Stupid me for creating this!', 'I'm so hopeless/inadequate/ugly/unlovable/selfish/neurotic.')*

❖ Telling yourself why you cannot have what you desire, or why you're not even allowed to want it – or trying to 'justify' your desire (which means you have contradictory beliefs)

❖ Believing you do not deserve to have what you want – that you are not good enough, or special enough, or perfect enough

❖ Giving in to others' needs, demands or expectations

❖ Becoming a sponge for others' negativity

Every time you fill yourself with negative thoughts – perhaps by listening to the news, reading the tabloids, or watching a grim documentary or tragic soap opera – you increase the negativity in the world, and attract more problems into your life. I remember a TV advert in which a well-known author was shown reading a quality newspaper, and saying 'If I read rubbish, I might start writing it.' The same is true of your mind. Turn your mind into a rubbish bin, and your life will start churning out rubbish. If you fill your thoughts with crisis, drama, illness, abuse, conflict, poverty, war, pain and tragedy, you begin to attract situations and events and people towards you that match those low vibrations. (For this reason, I haven't watched the news or read the papers for more than a decade.) The news does not 'keep you informed'; it mostly drip-feeds you with fear and victimhood, which disconnect you from your power. The law of attraction works for thoughts too, so thinking negatively means you attract more thoughts that match those vibrations – and it becomes a habit. Once you know that the outer world mirrors your inner world, you become much more choosy about what you watch, read or listen to, and the people you spend time with!

> *Change your thoughts, and you change your reality.*

The feel-good factor

Once you understand the law of attraction, you surround yourself with whatever gives you the feel-good factor. You fill your days with people and work and activities and places that make your heart sing. You create a home that feels relaxing and looks beautiful, and is filled with images of what you wish to create. You choose TV programmes, films and books that are inspiring and uplifting, which show you the beauty and joy in the world, which make you laugh, which lead you to reach out with love. You look for what is positive in others – for their strengths and talents and uniqueness – instead of criticising their perceived faults or inadequacies. You enjoy and honour ways in which others are different from you, valuing people's diversity. You feel gratitude for all that is good in your life, appreciating the moment-by-moment pleasures that make your days full and rich.

As a conscious dream-weaver, you never beat yourself up for having problems. As we shall see, problems are an essential ingredient in the broth of life; they help us to clarify what we really want, and launch a new future. So you accept what is, while reaching towards what might be. You notice any negative thoughts with self-love and gentleness, and let them go with a smile, soft as a breeze. Above all, you focus on what you desire. Like a child as Christmas approaches, you are full of joyful anticipation for the future. You just *know* that Christmas is coming, and your gifts are on their way! And in the meantime, look how wonderful life is!

Just for you

CHOOSING NEW THOUGHTS
Pick some aspect of your life – work, money, relationships, your home, health, your body, or any current problem that bothers you – and write down your usual thoughts about that subject. No editing. No censorship. Just note what you tend to believe

about that issue, or find yourself saying, or hear friends or family saying about the topic. Can you see how those thoughts and beliefs are mirrored back to you? Instead of telling yourself that you hold those beliefs because 'That is how it is', consider the possibility that 'That is how it is' because you hold those beliefs. Now find some more positive thoughts about this subject – thoughts or ideas or memories that feel soothing, reassuring, relieving, joyful or uplifting. Notice how those new thoughts make you feel. (Unless they change how you feel, you are not shifting your vibrations.)

GRATITUDE AND APPRECIATION

Every day, or as often as you remember, write a list of all you felt grateful for today. The letter from an old friend. A hug from your child. The sunshine. A delicious lunch. A warm smile from your neighbour. A walk in the park. The excitement of a new project at work. A stimulating conversation. The money in your bank account. Watching the sunset. A relaxing evening by a log fire. Even if something 'bad' happened, find a way of feeling grateful for it, or seeing it in a positive light. Throughout the day, pause to appreciate what is good and beautiful in this moment.

Keeping a gratitude journal – or simply making a constant habit of appreciation – can transform your life. It is one of the simplest and most powerful ways of raising your vibrations. As soon as I wake, I spend a few minutes focussing on all I feel grateful for in my life – and at the end of the day, as often as possible, I write down all that was wonderful in that particular day. Try book-ending your day with gratitude – and watch your life change.

Chapter Three

Feel Your Way into the Flow

*I believe that happiness is our natural state, that bliss is hardwired. **Candace Pert**[12]*

Let's suppose that you want to sell your house. If you have a clear vision of where you want to live next and why, and focus upon all that you have loved about the house, then the sale is likely to be smooth and rapid. The difficulty is that many people decide to sell their house because they are focussing on what is 'wrong' with it and why they want to get rid of it. (Kitchen too narrow. Street too noisy. Garden too small. Not enough storage space.) Or they dwell on what others might see as wrong with it. Or they listen to negativity about the current state of the housing market. Or explain to others *why* their house is not selling. Or focus on the faults and shortcomings of their estate agent. Or want to move so desperately that this becomes a blockage in itself – since we only feel desperate when we fear that our desires will not be met.

If you want to sell a house, make use of the law of attraction. Dwell on the positive. Make a list of all that you love and value about the house, and focus on these qualities. (At an energy level, anyone viewing the house will pick up these positive thoughts.) Appreciate all that your estate agent does for you – never criticise or complain, even silently – and enthuse about your house to them. See yourself moving to the new house of your dreams, and plan your life as if it has already been arranged. (The Universe *has* already organised this. Your task is to accept the gift.) Keep affirming all the reasons why someone would adore this house, and would happily pay the asking price. Let go of any negative thoughts with a gentle smile. If there is any action that you need to take – such as clearing clutter, washing the front door or re-painting the sitting room in magnolia – you will receive an intuitive impulse to do so. (After all, Source knows who your buyer will be, and what their tastes are!) Once you can think about selling your house and just feel a sense of joyful anticipation, without any niggling fears or doubts, you can relax. Forget about it. Your buyer is on the way!

Emotions as guidance

Perhaps the law of attraction sounds impersonal and uncaring. After all, it simply brings you whatever you focus upon, whether positive or negative. However, the cosmos is also set up to guide you towards your desires. The cosmos is not neutral or inert. This is a conscious and loving Universe – and it adores you. Yes, it adores you *personally*. Whatever you ask for, it always says yes, with no exceptions. Ask and it is given. What is more, it wants to deliver your gifts. So even if you are thinking negatively, the Universe keeps nudging you in the right direction. Whenever you focus upon what you do *not* want, or think there is something bad or wrong with you (or anyone else), you get a warning sign that your thoughts and desires are contradictory, that you are getting in your own way. Likewise, when your desires, beliefs and expectations are all consistent, so that you are attracting what you want, you get clear and positive feedback about this from Source energy – rather like a coach who is cheering you on from the sidelines. Helpful, hey?

So how do you get this guidance? Well, there is nothing tricky or esoteric to it. You don't have to sign up or pay for it. You don't need a priest, guru or teacher. You don't need to meditate for years to receive it. It might not be quite as obvious as a voice booming out of the sky, but it is ever-present. *Guidance comes through your emotions.* It is very simple and straightforward. If you feel good, what you desire is coming your way. If you feel bad, you are currently attracting what you do *not* want. You are disconnecting yourself from all the good things in life.

Emotions are our primary form of higher guidance – our direct phone line to Infinite Intelligence – and are central to making our dreams come true.

Your emotions are your higher guidance.

This is not what we have generally been taught about our emotions. Most of us have learnt to dismiss, suppress, ignore or deny our feelings – or to express them in ways that hold other people or circumstances responsible. ('You made me angry.' 'You disappointed me.' 'You hurt me.') Or we have been told to put others' feelings first. Or to pretend to be happy, regardless of how we feel. Emotions have been linked with our feminine side, so in a male-dominated culture they have not been taken seriously. Feelings have often been seen as mere distractions – misleading, unreliable and messy. I suspect this is because, once we grasp the true meaning and purpose of emotions, it is so empowering that it changes our lives. Like the wondrous secret of the law of attraction, this mystical knowledge has been suppressed until now.

Within the new world view, your emotions tell you whether Source energy – the creative force of the cosmos – is flowing freely through you. When you are feeling good, you are literally feeling the flow of God-force, which feels wonderful!

Feeling good (as opposed to *being* good in the eyes of others) is feeling God. *Feeling* good comes from seeing life as a gift, and therefore going with the flow; whereas *being*

good comes from a fear-based mythology which disconnects you from Source. Your emotions can be compared
with a ladder, in which your highest emotions are towards
the top of the ladder, and your lowest emotions are on
the bottom rungs. The higher up the ladder you are, the
more joyful and empowered you feel – and the more you
are going with the flow.

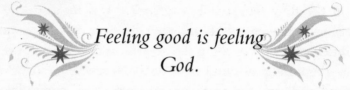

Feeling good is feeling God.

When Source is flowing through you, even doing the
washing up can be an ecstatic experience. (I remember
once being blissed out by the gleam on a white china
mug, amidst a rainbow of soap bubbles.) You feel fully
present in the moment, and this moment feels utterly
delicious. You are aligned with your higher self. You are a
fully embodied soul. But when you are disconnected from
Source, you might be walking in a beautiful landscape,
or making love, or hugging your child, and somehow it
doesn't *get through* to you. You cannot really enjoy and
appreciate it. You are just going through the motions. It is
as if you are living your life from a distance, and you feel
strangely empty and dissociated. (In fact, some people are
so habitually disconnected from Source that they engage
in life-threatening activities, or repeatedly attract melo-
drama, in order to feel alive at all.)

When you are fully in the flow, you feel joyful,
passionate, enthusiastic, inspired, fun-loving, grateful and
appreciative. When you feel good, that is the energy of

Love flowing through you. You love everyone and everything unconditionally, including yourself. You know that
you can have, do, or be anything that you want. You
feel vibrantly alive and present in the moment. You feel
zappy and energised. You are in touch with your intuitive knowing, and can trust any inner urges to take action
– knowing this will be the perfect time. At its best, being
in the flow feels totally orgasmic. (And making love –
at its best – is a fabulous way to connect with Source
energy, and the feeling of oneness.)

You will have your own signs that you're in the flow,
and it's worth noting what they are. When I'm in the flow,
my toes curl with delight, I smile and laugh readily, I see
beauty in everyone and everything, I am deeply sensual
and embodied, I reach out to people with an open heart,
I relax more, I read more poetry, I spend more time in
nature, I feel light-hearted and free, I am more creative,
and I find myself singing and dancing for no reason. In
short, I adore life!

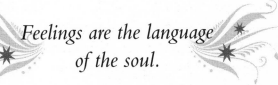

*Feelings are the language
of the soul.*

If you are well connected to Source energy, but just
slightly off-peak, you tend to feel peaceful, contented,
calm, patient, hopeful or maybe even optimistic. There is
a little less energy flowing through you, but life feels good.
You feel relaxed and accepting. The more you disconnect
from the flow – through negativity, fear or judgment –
the worse you feel. If you are mildly disconnected, you

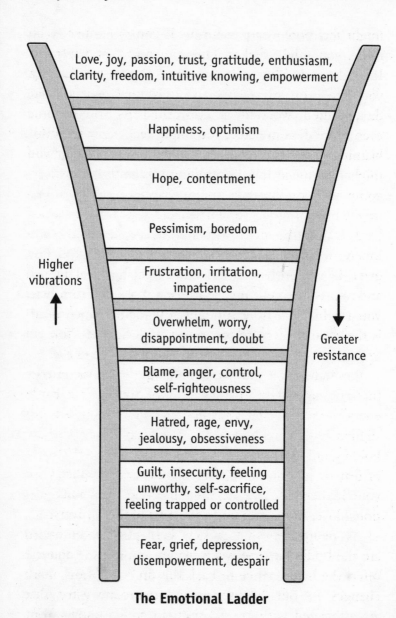

Love, joy, passion, trust, gratitude, enthusiasm, clarity, freedom, intuitive knowing, empowerment

Happiness, optimism

Hope, contentment

Pessimism, boredom

Frustration, irritation, impatience

Overwhelm, worry, disappointment, doubt

Blame, anger, control, self-righteousness

Hatred, rage, envy, jealousy, obsessiveness

Guilt, insecurity, feeling unworthy, self-sacrifice, feeling trapped or controlled

Fear, grief, depression, disempowerment, despair

Higher vibrations

Greater resistance

The Emotional Ladder

might feel bored or pessimistic. If you disconnect a bit more, you might feel irritated, impatient or frustrated. If you keep dwelling on what is bad or wrong or lacking, you head towards feeling overwhelmed, discouraged, disappointed, worried or concerned. As you become even more disconnected, you might feel angry, resentful, blaming or self-righteous. As you disconnect further, you might become jealous, controlling, mistrustful, suspicious, competitive or obsessive, or raging and vengeful – or you might be stoical and resigned. And if you have turned hard against the flow, you might feel guilty, insecure, lonely or self-sacrificing. At worst, you might feel fear, grief, depression, worthlessness or despair. You feel trapped and imprisoned, and unable to see a way out. From here, you might even have thoughts of suicide (since death is the ultimate way to reconnect with Source). You are at the bottom of your emotional ladder. You feel *bad*.[13]

Resistance is contradictory energy – that is, energy that goes against the natural flow of Source. It is battle energy. It means that your desires or intentions are not aligned with your beliefs and expectations, or you are holding unloving thoughts. You are listening to the voice of fear or judgment, and are therefore in conflict with your higher self. You are disconnecting from unconditional love, and saying no to the gifts of the Universe.

As neuroscientist Candace Pert puts it, emotions are the bodily link between matter and spirit – and she offers the hard science to back this up.[14] Emotions mark changes in our hormones and neurochemistry that are associated with crucial shifts in consciousness. Your emotions do not *create* your reality, but they do indicate what you are currently attracting. Our natural state is joy and bliss – and resistance means that you're not going with the flow, which is signalled to you by negative emotion. The heavier the resistance, the worse you feel. Your emotions are like traffic lights. Any positive emotion is a green signal which says 'Yes! You are moving towards your desires. Keep going!' Slight uneasiness or frustration is an amber light; you are in no-man's-land, sending out some contradictory signals, neither moving towards nor away from your desires. Negative emotion is a red warning light: 'Stop – you are going in the wrong direction. Turn around.'

> *When you feel bad, you are saying no to the gifts of the Universe.*

You are never alone, even in your darkest hours. If you feel any negative emotion or discomfort, that is Source speaking to you. Feelings are the language of the soul. Love is always there, moment by moment, calling you to reconnect – holding its hand in yours, and whispering softly in your ear. *You only feel bad because the Universe is trying to help you*. It is warning you that your current thoughts are short-circuiting your energy flow. You are disconnecting from Love. You are turning your back on your dreams. Time to turn around. Time to wake up. Any thought that feels uncomfortable is not aligned with who you really are, or with your desires. It is coming from a fearful part of you – which is doing its best from its limited and split-off perspective, but cannot think like the Universe.

If you keep ignoring negative emotion, your resistance might turn into chronic anxiety, depression or physical symptoms, as well as appearing in the outer world in situations that you will not enjoy. (An unexpected bill arrives, your boss shouts at you, the washing machine floods your kitchen, you get a speeding fine – or worse.) Then you feel even worse. So unless you want life to be stuck or painful, your task is to release any resistance. Your task is to feel your way into the flow.

If you go with the flow, whatever you desire will come to you – since that is how the Universe is designed. You do not need to label an emotion; you just need to know whether it feels good. Your emotions indicate your current vibrations. Feeling bad indicates low vibrations – or high resistance – which means you are getting in your own way. Feeling good indicates high vibrations – low resistance – which means you are allowing the Universe to deliver your gifts to you. It is as simple as that. (And there is no limit to joy and ecstasy. However good you feel, you can feel even better – which means you enjoy life even more, and attract even more miracles.)

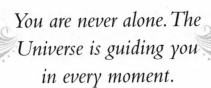

You are never alone. The Universe is guiding you in every moment.

The best metaphor I've come across for emotional guidance is satellite navigation.[15] If you ask a car's satellite navigation system to guide you towards a chosen destination, it gives you precise directions, turn by turn. It simply notes where you are right now, and where you desire to be, and works out the best route. It does not question whether your chosen destination is desirable, or whether you are *allowed* to go there, or whether anyone else *wants* you to go there. It never says you cannot get there from here. It does not ask where you were last week, or in your childhood (or even in a past life), in order to chart your route. It simply notes where you are, and where you want to be – and guides you towards it. If you take a detour or make a wrong turning, it gives you fresh instructions so that you get back on track, or re-calculates your route afresh. No problem. And your emotional guidance works in exactly the same way. It pinpoints where you are, and where you want to be. Then it guides you step by step. Thought by thought. Moment by moment. And if you just focus on *feeling good* – on following your emotional guidance, instead of listening to guidance from anyone or anywhere else – you will reach your chosen destination. (But you do have to tell it where you want to go, or nothing will happen!)

Becoming a conscious co-creator

The principles of reality creation are simple:

✧ Ask and it is given

✧ Nothing can block you except *your* resistance

✧ You get what you focus upon

✧ Feel your way into the flow

✧ Once you're in the flow, your dreams will come true

Putting these principles into practice is more intricate – but only because we are still wrestling with the old mindset of conditional love. Our old habits of thought. The world of fear and victimhood. From the old, child-like mythology which sees life as a trial, you might imagine that God will take pity on you if you are miserable enough, or have worked hard or suffered or sacrificed yourself enough. You expect to feel good once a problem is resolved, or you have what you want, or other people or circumstances change. But that is conditional love. Reality does not operate like that. You are a co-creator with the cosmos. (This is why any prayer that comes from complete faith and trust will – by the law of attraction – be answered. Equally, any prayer that comes from a sense of lack, fear or desperation cannot be answered.) The Universe offers emotional guidance so that you can feel your way back into the flow – but it cannot send you new and happy conditions if you are thinking the same old fearful, guilt-ridden, despairing or resentful thoughts. Nothing changes until you do.

From the new world view, the paradox is that you have to change how you think and feel *first*. You have to trust your emotional guidance – knowing that if you feel good, your gifts are on their way. You have to love and honour yourself, accept your starting point and focus on what you want from here. As you step more and more into the new world view, based on unconditional love and empowerment, you become invincible. You are thinking like the Universe. Then you become a god or goddess who can transform lead into gold.

However, it is important to be patient. It takes a while for reality to catch up with your vibrations – thanks to the helpful buffer of time. You need to hold new desires, beliefs and expectations for a while before reality comes into line. Your energy needs to be stable and coherent, like a laser beam. If you keep wobbling between positive and negative thoughts about a desire, then you delay it coming, or might create what you want, then lose it again. We see this in one-hit wonders who rise to stardom, then quickly fade into obscurity; or someone who wins the lottery, squanders it all and slides into bankruptcy; or when a woman finds the partner of her dreams, then he dies or leaves her.

Passionate and intense desire can bring what you want – but if you tell yourself it is 'too good to be true', or that you are not good enough or don't deserve it, then you cannot hold on to your dream. It is much better to stabilise your vibrations *before* it happens – by holding on to positive beliefs and expectations, letting go of any resistance and *slowly* feeling your way into the flow. This is why patience can be a virtue! Then when your dream does come true, it will feel natural and what-is-to-be-expected. It will perfectly match your new vibrations. (And since you have to focus on *something*, it is wise to focus on your dreams and desires, and what you appreciate. Unless we have a positive and creative focus, we tend to ruminate on problems, illness or bad news.)

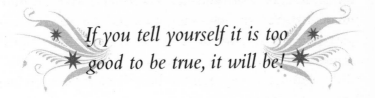

If you tell yourself it is too good to be true, it will be!

If you can think about any subject and consistently feel wonderful, then your dream is on its way. That is guaranteed. You can get an instant litmus test on any issue by turning your attention to it. Think about money in your life, for example. Does it make you feel happy, powerful, excited and free – or just relaxed and at peace? If so, you can be sure that whatever you desire financially is on its way – or that the healthy state of your finances is stable. But if the word 'money' makes you feel anxious, hopeless, trapped, depressed, guilty, resigned, envious, irritable, frustrated or out of control, your emotional guidance is warning you that your habitual thoughts about money are leading you away from what you desire. You have been warned! Money is just energy, and there is no limit to energy. The only question is how freely you allow that energy we call money to flow into your life. The flow of money will perfectly mirror your feelings and beliefs about it.

The great news is that because we live in an energy-based reality, you only need to change your thoughts and you begin to attract new realities. You are not dependent upon anyone or anything 'out there' changing. You might imagine that your future depends upon whether an interview panel decides in your favour, or the doctor gives you a clean bill of health, or the bank manager says yes to a business loan or mortgage, or even whether you win the lottery – but all of those circumstances depend entirely upon *you*. Your thoughts. Your vibrations. Whether you can align your desires with your beliefs and expectations. Life is always a dance of co-creation, so no one else can 'do' anything to you. You invite it all.

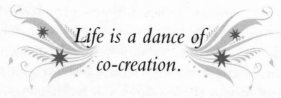

Life is a dance of co-creation.

A word of warning: winning the lottery is too much of a quantum leap up the emotional ladder for most people. You can only raise your vibrations by a rung or two at a time – which is why using joyful affirmations is a waste of time while you are lodged in fear, guilt or depression. Shaking your fist at God or the cosmos, or your boss, or partner – or throwing that annoying book of affirmations across the room – might work better! If you're near the bottom of the ladder, joy is so far beyond your current vibrations that it is like reaching for the moon, and happy people who are bouncing around like Tiggers are likely to seem irritating rather than uplifting.

Also, not many people can *believe* that they will win the lottery, since the rational mind keeps throwing the unlikely statistics at us! If you're waiting to win the lottery, you are likely to wait forever. It is far more efficient to send out a desire for prosperity, then ask the Universe to find some way of delivering it to you. In the meantime, start *feeling* your way into prosperity. Hang out with wealthy people. Read about the rich and famous, and imagine yourself in their shoes. Focus on all the positive reasons why you want more money. Feel grateful for the money you do have. Release any thoughts of envy or resentment, or feeling trapped by your low income, or any belief that if you have less, others have more. As far as possible, don't do anything 'just for the money', since this reinforces your belief in shortage and lack. Let go of any negative thoughts about money or wealth – and life-is-a-trial mythology is full of these – until you can think about money and feel great! Money is just energy; it is limitless. And it can come to you in many different ways – as long as you are not sending out contradictory signals.

Similarly, if you want to find a soul mate, don't limit yourself by asking for a relationship with a *specific* person – though it is fine to imagine someone specific, then say 'I'd love to be with this person for these reasons, *or with someone like this.*' Always leave it up to Infinite Intelligence – which knows everyone on the planet intimately, and sees all possible futures – to set up the necessary circumstances and events. Once you are in the flow, you will find yourself in the right place at the right time with the right person. It might or might not be the person you expected. This is where trust comes in, and letting go of control. Never pin down the Universe! It knows far more than you do.

The forces of the Universe are always on your side.

Everything that you experience comes from your vibrations, which are signalled by your emotions. Once you understand the true purpose of your emotions, you will never again tolerate or deny negative emotions, nor squash them with food, work, exercise or busyness. You will be exquisitely sensitive to any sign of tension, to that twinge or discomfort in your solar plexus, to that anxiety or guilt or resentment, or sense of deflation or discouragement, and take corrective action – not by trying to control other people or events or circumstances, but by changing your *inner* world.

Let me clarify the difference between conditional and unconditional love – since this is central to reality creation. (And to our happiness and freedom.) Conditional love says 'I will be happy as long as I enjoy what I am seeing or experiencing.' If you feel bad, conditional love wants to control and manipulate other people or circumstances so that you feel better. This never works, since what you see 'out there' (or even in your body) simply matches your vibrations; it is feedback about the radio signals you are giving out. Unconditional love says 'My happiness is my responsibility, and I will change myself rather than trying to control other people or events.' *Then* the conditions 'out there' will change – or you might see them differently, or flow effortlessly towards new decisions, relationships or circumstances – since your vibrations have changed.

continued ...

The paradox is that if you change yourself *in order* to change other people or the world, your love is still conditional. That is still being manipulative. You have to change because aligning yourself with Source is what matters most – because, above all, you want to think like your higher self. Then nothing can perturb you, or not for long, since you are in charge of your own happiness. Then you are truly free. Your happiness no longer depends upon other people or circumstances – and you let everyone else off the hook.

My happiness is my own responsibility. I let everyone else off the hook.

Whatever happens, you can choose negative, blaming and disempowering thoughts – based on conditional love – such as 'This has ruined my life.' 'How could she have done that to me?' 'I behaved so badly.' 'He betrayed me.' 'I was so stupid.' Or you can choose positive, loving and empowering thoughts – 'I've learnt so much from this, and can move on now.' 'She mirrored back my beliefs perfectly.' 'I understand why I behaved that way.' 'I understand why he behaved that way.' Even if the event is as minor as being late for an appointment, choose thoughts that are loving and reassuring instead of blaming someone else, or (even worse) beating yourself up! It's crucial to realise that this isn't 'just' making you feel better. The point is that nothing is more important than how you feel. Feeling better means that you are attracting a different future. When you live in the world of Love, not only do you feel great, but you attract whatever you desire. Life gets better and better.

From the world of unconditional love, you also *interpret* events differently. Nothing can threaten you. If someone makes a barbed remark, it simply glides off your shoulder since there is nothing for it to stick to: 'They are probably having a bad day.' When a friend doesn't phone as arranged, you might think 'They were probably busy, or just forgot. No big deal.' If you are feeling unhappy or insecure, however, you are more likely to *make* it a big deal. 'Perhaps they had an accident.' 'Maybe I've upset them.' 'He probably never liked me anyway.' 'I bet she never speaks to me again.' When your vibrations are low, you can twist and distort almost any event, and choose the worst possible interpretation. The most innocent remark cuts you like a knife. You over-react to the mildest criticism or rebuff. You take everything personally. You make wild accusations that leave others bewildered. You suspect that a twinge in your head signals a brain tumour. You make a mountain out of every molehill. Then other people react to your negativity, and you bring out the worst in them – or they tread on eggshells around you, or try to avoid you. You get caught in a downward spiral, and any action that you take from there will be self-defeating – *until* you pay attention to your emotional guidance.

*Nothing is more important
than how you feel.*

Climbing the emotional ladder

So how do you find your way into the flow? By believing in a Universe based upon unconditional love, in which you do not have to earn or deserve love, or anything else that you desire. By knowing that life is a gift. By loving and appreciating all that is good in your life. By seeing everyone and everything in a positive light. By loving and appreciating yourself. By making peace with What Is – and telling yourself positive stories about it. By reassuring and accepting yourself when you are out of the flow. By allowing yourself to be human, and laughing more. By not trying so hard. By not comparing yourself to others. By nurturing and caring for yourself. By being playful and having fun. By choosing to be happy rather than trying to be good. By following your bliss. By reaching out with love. By meditating (which releases resistance). By believing in your dreams. By happily daydreaming about what you desire. By letting yourself off the hook, and treating life as a vacation. By chilling out, relaxing more and breathing deeply. By choosing thoughts and memories and experiences that make you feel good. By doing less and less that you 'must', 'ought' or 'should' do, and more and more that makes your heart sing and your spirit dance. Above all, by trusting your emotional guidance – knowing that nothing is more important than feeling good.

I picture the emotional ladder as shaped like a fan – narrow at the bottom, and wide at the top – since this is how it *feels*. When you are at the bottom of the ladder, it feels like being stuck in a broom cupboard. You feel trapped and stuck, and your thoughts are limited and repetitive. It feels tight and claustrophobic. As you climb higher and higher, you feel more and more expansive and free – as if you are moving into lighter and more spacious rooms, then flowing out into the gardens and (near the top) into the breadth of the cosmos. You see a bigger and bigger picture. Your dreams and visions expand.

> *As you climb the emotional ladder, you feel more and more free.*

Happily, you don't have to reach the top of the emotional ladder before you feel good. As soon as you're moving in the right direction, you immediately feel better. Releasing resistance always feels like a relief. Just choosing a thought that is *slightly* higher on the emotional ladder allows more energy to flow through you. You can breathe more deeply. You relax and soften a little. You feel liberated. You are no longer pushing against the flow.

ANGER AND THE EMOTIONAL LADDER
I remember attending a shamanic workshop many years ago, in which we were asked to express any unresolved anger. Many people were thumping cushions, shouting

expletives at long-dead relatives, screaming with rage – and clearly liberated by it. They were releasing resistance. But my emotions were hovering between joy and optimism at that time, so reaching for anger would have lowered my vibrations. Along with a few others, I stood uneasily at the edge of the room, unable to enter into the exercise. If I had felt disempowered at that time, anger might have felt good and energised me.

Whether any emotion feels good is always relative to your starting point. If you are feeling hopeful, say, then anger would lower your vibrations and feel bad. But if you feel shame, guilt, fear, helplessness or despair, feeling angry is one step closer to Love. It will release resistance and feel good. I often joke that if you ever have a choice between blaming yourself or blaming someone else, always choose someone else! Just for now. Whenever you feel guilty or disempowered, anger or blame is a good temporary choice from there – and you know it is, because it makes you *feel better*. It is a move towards self-respect and empowerment. It is a step in the right direction. (The reason why thoughts of shame or guilt feel so awful is that they are a million miles from how your higher self thinks – since it loves you without condition, and never sees any fault, imperfection or wrongdoing.)

> *Negative emotion always comes from feeling disempowered.*

All too often, people slip from anger back into guilt or depression. If you feel angry or resentful, then tell yourself it is bad or wrong to feel angry – that nasty people get angry while nice people feel guilty, or that you create your own reality so it is all your 'fault' – then you will plummet down the ladder again. Or others might react to your anger with criticism or defensiveness, and you feel ashamed and guilty. You feel worse. Then you remind yourself that they really *did* hurt you, behave unreasonably or ignore your feelings – which makes you feel a bit better – and you fire yourself up with anger again. You can then flip endlessly between anger/blame and guilt/powerlessness in an exhausting spiral. Judging yourself or judging others. Some people do this for years and years!

There is an alternative to whirling in circles at the bottom of the emotional ladder. You can enjoy the relief of feeling angry for a while, then keep going with the flow *beyond anger* – noticing what thoughts feel better from there. Then you can climb the ladder from anger towards frustration or irritation. As you climb more rungs of the ladder, you can see farther and get a bigger perspective. You move beyond judgment. From there, you might be able to see the funny side of it, or find some hopeful thoughts or helpful insights – such as understanding how you created what is happening through the law of attraction. (Not beating yourself up for this, but with a sense of curiosity and satisfaction.) Or listening to the other person, and realising they simply have different needs or values, or were feeling hurt or confused themselves, and were not behaving badly from *their* perspective. After all, everyone is good and loving at heart. When you find such thoughts, you are thinking like the Universe. You find yourself smiling. You are becoming your higher self. The sun is shining through.

> *When you think like the Universe, you find yourself smiling.*

Falling in love with life

Paradoxically, when you are self-centred enough to follow your emotional guidance, you become more and more kind and loving. Why? Firstly, because you are climbing out of the world of fear and judgment, and rising into the world of unconditional love. You see everyone and everything through rose-coloured eyes. You fall in love with life. Secondly, because when you value yourself enough to honour your own emotions and needs, you are far more resourceful. You can give to others from a full cup, instead of scrabbling to give from a cup that is nearly empty. Those who give from a sense of unworthiness or insecurity – from trying to *earn* love and approval – tend to become depressed, resentful and exhausted. When you give because you are overflowing with love and joy, you never feel depleted, since you are constantly replenishing yourself. Your cup is always full. You are connected to Source energy. You have so much more to give – and you are also open to receive. You feel secure, worthy and self-assured. Then the cosmos can shower you with its gifts.

Last night, as I tucked my gorgeous son into bed, he looked up and said, 'I love you so much. This is a happy life. I love *everything* about my life.' What a wonderful example of going with the flow! Love, appreciation and acceptance of What Is. Once you're in the flow, you hardly care whether your current dreams and desires will come true, since you feel fabulous anyway! Life feels great; and it just gets better and better. And when you have felt consistently in the flow for a while, you know that you are aligned with Source – and you can trust that your dreams *are* on their way. It is guaranteed.

Just for you

BEING YOUR OWN BEST FRIEND
Whether you are pondering a major decision, or simply choosing what to do today, try asking yourself: If I loved myself uncondi- tionally, what would I do right now? If I knew that I could trust my own feelings and desires, what would I do? If I knew that I was safe and loved, what would I choose? If I knew that there are no wrong choices, what would I do? If I knew there was nothing to fear, what would I choose? If I ignored others' needs or opin- ions, what would I do? If I allowed myself to be wild and free, what would my choice be? These are questions that help you slip free from fear or judgment, and feel your way into the flow. Then you are free to be who you really are. (Keeping a private journal of your innermost feelings, musings and reflections can help you stay in touch with your authentic self – the deeper self that lies beyond your socially conditioned self, or what others expect from you.) If you become aware of any niggling voice of anxiety or guilt or self-doubt, imagine wrapping your arms around that child-like self, and reassuring it that it is safe and loved.

FOLLOWING YOUR BLISS

Become sensitive to how you feel – to your vibrations – when you focus on any issue, or as you go about your day. How do you feel right now? And now? And now? Where might you place yourself on your emotional ladder? If you notice any dip in your emotions, don't beat yourself up for it. Accept it – or you remain stuck. Love yourself anyway. Notice what thoughts made you slip down a rung or two. Then find some way of easing back up. Relax. Follow your bliss. Choose more positive thoughts. Read an inspirational book. Be appreciative. Daydream. Dance. Laugh. Stroke your cat. Hug your partner. Make love. Go jogging. Take a walk in nature. Or silently rage against someone, if that makes you feel good right now! Do whatever it takes to find the glorious sense of relief that comes as you feel your way into the flow.

Prepare a Bliss List of activities that make you feel good, so that you have a handy list to refer to. Make sure you prioritise what is on this list each day – and use your Bliss List whenever you feel out of the flow. Remember: nothing is more important than feeling good.

Chapter Four

The Inner Voice
of Love

Love has nothing to do with sacrifice.
Paul Ferrini[16]

When my son was younger, I often read him a bedtime
story about three little wolves and a big bad pig. Before
they left home, the three little wolves were warned by
their mother about the big bad pig. So they built a house
of bricks to protect themselves from the pig. When the
big bad pig knocked down their house with a sledge
hammer, the wolves built an even stronger home made
of concrete. The pig used a pneumatic drill to break in.
The frightened little wolves then barricaded themselves

into a grim, grey house of armour plates, iron bars and padlocks, surrounded by barbed wire. But the pig blew *that* up with dynamite. At last, the wolves realised they must be moving in the wrong direction – so they built their next house from flowers, and slender branches of wood. It was fragile but beautiful. Along came the big bad pig, and smelt the sweet and fragrant flowers. He breathed in deeply. His heart opened, and he began to dance with joy. The wolves and the big pig all became friends, and lived happily ever after.[17]

This story is a metaphor for the current journey of humanity – through increasing fear and separation, until we wake up and shift into unconditional love and oneness. Like the little wolves, you cannot feel safe while you are living in fear, no matter how much you try to protect yourself. You will only prove to yourself that your fears were justified, since low vibrations attract negative experiences. Focus on what is bad or wrong or dangerous, and you will *create* big bad pigs or big bad wolves! Listen to your fearful and protective mother, and you learn fearful habits of thought. Unite with anyone against a common 'enemy', and it keeps you trapped in fear and insecurity. It is only when you *let down* your defences that you find true safety and inner peace. You move beyond the world of duality – the world of good and bad, right and wrong, safe and dangerous – and connect with the natural love and goodness of the cosmos.

The more you protect yourself, the more vulnerable you become.

'But there *are* dangers in the world!' you might protest. 'There are big bad wolves, and runaway cars, and bombs and terrorists, and thugs and robbers, and unscrupulous people...'. But you will not come into contact with them when you are in the flow. The flow would never take you there. 'But what if I get it wrong? What if I'm not in the flow? I must watch out just in case!' But that voice of anxiety and mistrust immediately takes you out of the flow. If you are protecting yourself, you are cutting yourself off from the unswerving love and grace of the Universe, which will always guide you to where you need to be, and what you need to do.

These two worlds of fear and love correspond to fear-based and love-based cosmologies respectively. Everyone has the capacity to live in either world – which gives you very different thoughts, and attracts very different realities. The more you learn to trust your emotions, and feel your way into the flow, the more you connect with the expansive world of unconditional love. Then you become your higher self – and can create anything that you desire.

Fear-mode and love-mode

The pioneering biologist Bruce Lipton has found that the cells in your body are always in one of two modes:

protection or growth.[18] This corresponds emotionally to fear or love. That is, your emotions indicate whether you are physiologically in fear-mode (focussing on perceived threats, closing down and giving knee-jerk reactions) or love-mode (feeling safe, and reaching-out, opening, connecting and expanding). In other words, every cell has the capacity to switch between two worlds: the world of fear or the world of love. A loving and co-operative creation myth or a battle-ridden cosmology. *In response to your thoughts*, they bow down to the old god of fear and judgment, and live in a world of fear and struggle, in which you must be good, and danger and evil must be fought off or kept at bay. Or your cells can expand into a world beyond fear and defensiveness – a creative world of unconditional love and joy and freedom, in which your dreams can (and will) come true.

Fear makes us hold back and contract. Love makes us reach out and expand.

REACTING FROM FEAR-MODE

Whenever we feel threatened or judged, we tend to flip into protection mode. Danger! Red alert! Emergency! This is a defensive and habitual mode that takes you out of the flow, and separates you from Love. From fear-mode, you react from your primitive or reptilian brain – which limits your behaviour to fight, flight or freeze. Your body floods with adrenaline. You feel mistrustful and on guard. You are imprisoned by fear, even panic – like a rabbit caught in headlights. You exclude or withdraw from anyone or anything that feels bad or dangerous. You seek control and security. You are afraid of change, so you tend to repeat the same old patterns. You feel empty and lonely, since you are disconnecting from Source – which makes you vulnerable to addictions and co-dependency. Your consciousness is walled off and constricted. It is hard to think clearly, make decisions or plan for the future. You are caught up in negative loops of thought which go round and round in circles. You develop tunnel vision, and no longer feel free to choose. You slip into playing roles – such as wife, mother, daughter, husband, brother, father, nurse, accountant, teacher or neighbour – and cannot risk being authentic and spontaneous.

Being in fear-mode is like falling asleep, and going on auto-pilot. You lose your depth, richness and creativity. Your spiritual awareness fades – and your mental and physical health are at risk. Like Sleeping Beauty, you are locked in a glass coffin, waiting for the kiss that will awaken you.

When you flip into fear-mode, you will have characteristic ways of coping with your anxiety, and trying to feel safe and loved:

✥ You might blame, attack, criticise, control or manipulate others – seeing them as in the wrong. *(Fight.)*

✥ You might try hard to please, give in, accommodate to others and do whatever is expected. *(Flight.)*

✧ You might close down or withdraw, in order to feel safe. *(Freeze.)*

✧ Or you might try to reconnect with Source – to fill your emptiness – through work, shopping, exercise or other driven, compulsive behaviours. *(Addiction.)*

Whatever you do, you will feel uneasy at best – because you are disconnecting from Love. You are being defensive and self-protective, and seeing the problem as 'out there'. You are not being guided by your emotions. You are not listening to the ever-present call of Source – which always calls you towards joy and freedom and expansion.

Being in fear-mode is thoroughly bad news. It is the reason why 'bad things happen to good people'. When you are in fear-mode, negative emotion will be warning you that you are currently sabotaging your own desires. You are attracting what you do not want – since your thoughts are focussed on the negative, or you are trying to earn or deserve love. And you will be unable to climb far up the emotional ladder until you release some resistance, and shift into love-mode.

Fear makes you feel separated from Love. No one can feel insecure or vulnerable or unloved while connected to Source. No one can be cruel or unkind while connected to Source. No one can feel a sense of lack or shortage while connected to Source. Unkindness, cruelty, envy, righteousness, aggression, greed, jealousy, competition, rage and revenge – as well as guilt, shame or feeling disempowered – all come from being in fear-mode.

Crucially, when your cells are switched into fear-mode,

there is no growth – biologically or psychologically. Defensiveness is a form of resistance. So the longer you stay in protection, the more you compromise your personal and spiritual growth. Being in fear-mode might mean you avoid change or risk, guard yourself against danger, and restrict your life to repetitive routines. From fear-mode, relationships remain shallow and unfulfilling, or controlling and dependent. You might feel characteristically 'bound by loyalty' to dysfunctional relationships or situations, remaining stuck for years on end.[19]

Being in fear-mode can mean that you secretly postpone life or happiness until some future date – when you fall in love, when you have moved house, when you have finished your degree, when the children go to school, when the children have left home, when you are married or divorced, when you have retired, when you have more money, or when you are less committed and busy. Deep down, you know that life is supposed to be more than this – but you paddle in the shallows, waiting for the right time to swim out into the ocean. After all, there might be sharks out there! Meanwhile the years drift past …

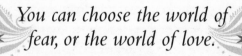

You can choose the world of fear, or the world of love.

How easily we feel threatened, and shift into the world of fear, seems to depend largely upon our childhood experiences. Any form of emotional, physical or sexual abuse, bullying, neglect, abrupt separation or trauma – or having parents, caretakers or teachers who were anxious,

judgmental or steeped in the old religions – can make us feel
unsafe or unloved. (So this includes almost everyone.) The
more fear or judgment you grew up with, the more protection becomes a customary way of being.[20] You flip into it
readily. It feels family-ar from childhood. It becomes a habit
to look out for threats, to close down, to attack or defend,
to be over-inhibited or controlling, to avoid conflict, to
seek safety or approval, to avoid guilt rather than choosing
happiness. But as you do this, your vibrations tumble down
the emotional ladder. Your awareness contracts. You feel
embattled. You slip into self-sabotage – and cannot reach
the higher echelons of love and joy and inner peace.

SWITCHING INTO LOVE-MODE

The good news is that fear is just denied love – just as darkness is merely absence of light. Another reality is waiting
for you. Once you see the world as safe and loving, or you
are in the presence of a truly loving relationship, you relax
into another mode of being. Your body releases endor-
phins, the pleasure hormones. Your higher brain comes
into operation. Then you feel free to make personal and
creative choices. You feel more expansive and liberated.
You feel trusting and open. You feel relaxed and at peace.
There is no need for defensiveness, so you can be honest
with others and true to yourself. You can listen without
feeling threatened. Love pours in and flows out freely.
You are connected to Source energy. Your consciousness
expands, and a whole new world opens up. And this is
how humanity is evolving; this is the new awareness we
are rapidly moving towards. It is our natural mode of
being, once we release our resistance.

Love is our natural mode of being.

With every thought, you are operating from fear or love. Separation or connectedness. Stagnation or flow. Protection or growth. Judgment or acceptance. Insecurity or self-worth. Criticism or appreciation. Closing down or opening up. Conformity or freedom. Control or trust. Dusty old habits, or fresh new desires. Everyone has the innate capacity to inhabit either of these worlds. These two states of awareness seem to be built into our physiology as well as our psychology. And when you expand into the world of love, the Universe can easily fulfil your dreams.

To thine own self be true

Imagine someone who truly loves you – someone who never withdraws their love, whatever you say or think or feel, however you behave. Someone who understands you completely, and loves you just as you are. Someone who sees your true potential, and is always rooting for you. Someone who makes no demands, other than wanting you to fulfil your desires and be true to yourself. In their eyes, you could never do any wrong. You are a wondrous being of light. Whether or not you have a personal relationship like this right now – whether with a partner, parent or friend – you still have access to unconditional love, because Source loves you in this way. This is what love really means. And when you connect with this inner voice of Love, it can transform your life.

> *You are deeply loved and cherished by the Universe.*

In the film *Billy Elliot*, the young hero is growing up in a rough, working-class culture in a mining family crippled by bereavement, threatened redundancy and financial hardship. A dark future seems to lie ahead. Unhappy with his father's harsh choice of boxing lessons, Billy secretly signs up for a ballet class – and soon discovers that dancing brings him alive. It brings him into the flow. Billy has found his passion, his vision, his true vocation. He longs to become a dancer. Eventually his father discovers what has been going on, and is outraged. Ballet is a shameful and inappropriate choice for a boy! He clamps down on his non-conformist son, and asserts his own authority and control. But with the support of a determined mentor, Billy holds onto his dream – and slowly wins over his struggling family. Love, warmth, hope and pride begin to flow again. Eventually he gains a place at the Royal Ballet School, and a glittering future beckons.

Not everyone has a burning vocation like young Billy – but we all face times when we are torn between honouring our own dreams, or meeting others' needs and expectations – being true to ourselves, or seeking approval. Being honest and authentic, or fitting in and conforming. At turning points in our lives, such choices can mean agonising dilemmas that affect our whole future.

Conformity is the plague of the fear-based cosmologies. But once you understand the laws of the cosmos, you will always follow your heart. You will honour your holy longing to express yourself, and reach for your wildest dreams. You will know that when anyone sacrifices themselves, *everyone* loses. In a Universe based upon unconditional love, love never means making sacrifices. You can have, do and be anything that you want. The Universe calls you to love yourself *without condition*. Once you trust your emotional guidance, you will follow the ancient dictum: 'To thine own self be true' – which means listening to the inner voice of Love.

As psychologist Marshall Rosenberg notes, 'Depression is the reward you get for being good.'[21] Giving in to others is a slow form of suicide. It might sound benign to please others – but you cannot be good *and* be authentic. You are pretending to be someone you are not. You are hiding your true feelings and desires. You feel held back, restrained and inhibited. You are tamed and driven by fear. You are trapped in the bottom half of the emotional ladder. If you care more about what others think than about how you feel, you will always be separated from your higher self. At best, trying to be good and perfect might make you feel virtuous. But seeking approval never leads to joy or passion or creativity. Approval is conditional love; it comes from fear-mode. It blocks your dreams – and makes true love and intimacy impossible.

If you care more about what others might think than about how you feel, you will never live a life that belongs to you.

Relationships are the source of our deepest pleasure and joy, but also our greatest pain and heartache. And most of this pain comes from love being conditional – which means you are trying to be good, or expecting others (or the world) to be good *in your eyes*. If you divide the world into good and bad, you only have two options. You can see the 'badness' within yourself and try to repress, hide or deny it, while secretly feeling ashamed, guilty and not good enough. (*Very* uncomfortable.) Or you can project the badness or inadequacy on to the outside world – and become controlling, critical, resentful, smug or self-righteous. (Slightly less uncomfortable.)

Most of us learnt to be 'good' in childhood, and to tuck away whatever was seen as unacceptable – perhaps anger, greed, jealousy, exuberance, sexuality, creativity or spirituality. Those split-off parts of the self become your dark and light Shadow. When you later see parts of your Shadow in the world, it makes you feel uneasy, irritable, angry, uncomfortable, insecure or threatened. Or you might admire, envy or fall in love with the other person. Anyone who brings up strong feelings – negative or positive – is a clue to some aspect of you that has been tamed and suppressed, and is calling for attention. It might be a part that has been punished or disapproved of when it has emerged in the past, or a desire or impulse that scares or excites you when it bubbles up. The more you squash or deny any part of yourself, the more likely it is to materialise in outer reality. Sooner or later, you will probably attract a relationship or situation that challenges you to embrace those lost parts of yourself – which is an opportunity to become more whole, to love yourself without condition.

Beyond blame and guilt

While you see anyone else as the problem, or are waiting for *them* to change, you are stuck. You are seeing the problem as outside you. And you're likely to create a similar challenge with someone else, and someone else, and someone else, until you get the message. After all, you create your own reality. If you feel disempowered, or a victim of others' behaviour, you are giving your power away. No one has the power to do anything to you. No one else can keep you out of the flow, no matter what they are doing.

No one else can keep you out of the flow. Only you.

The cosmic joke is that you are pulling the strings. No one can tread on your toes unless you have 'invited' them – at a vibrational level – to do so. The more you push against anyone – whether it is a meddling in-law, troublesome ex, demanding boss, rebellious teenager or noisy neighbour – the more they will push back at you. See the worst in anyone, and that is what they will show you. Eventually you might be barricading your doors and windows in your attempts to keep out the big bad pig – but it is all your own creation! You are listening to the voice of fear, instead of the voice of Love. Rather than analysing what is wrong with them, look at yourself. It is *you* who needs to grow and change. (Which does not mean there is anything wrong with you. Just negative habits of thinking.)

Even if it is as simple as your partner snoring, if you keep affirming and complaining about it, the snoring will get worse! If you feel controlled or rejected by someone, you invited that, or you are interpreting their behaviour in that way. The more you see a colleague as lazy or nit-picking, the more lazy or nit-picking he or she will become – at least in your presence. The more you object to passive smoking, the more you will attract smokers around you wherever you go. The more you have to 'justify' ending a relationship by proving how awful your ex-partner is, the more they will continue to prove it!

The Universe responds entirely to your vibrations. This is not a solid reality that is separate from you, but an energetic tapestry. The outer world always mirrors back your thoughts, your beliefs, your expectations. Again, this is not a reason for blaming yourself or beating yourself up; it is all about self-empowerment and response-ability.

Fear and love cannot be held in the same breath. Choose fear, and you step out of the flow. Choose love, and the flow carries you wherever you want to go. You cannot be righteous *and* happy. (Feeling righteous *or* guilty means you are seeing someone as in the wrong – which your higher self would never do.) Once you recognise what you are splitting off – and heal yourself – it is remarkable how often those scary, difficult or irritating people tend to change, disappear or no longer bother you. Once you look for the best in someone, they can reveal it to you. Or you feel able to talk with them openly and honestly – without blame, guilt or defensiveness.

You can be righteous – or you can be happy.

Beyond forgiveness

Does this mean you should forgive anyone who has hurt you? If you want to move beyond anger and blame, yes. If you want to stop feeling like a victim, yes. If you want to find inner peace, yes. If you want to be in the flow, yes. If you want to stop attracting similar situations in future, yes. Forgiveness means letting go of resentment, and releasing yourself from the past. It sets you free. But forgiveness is only a first step towards your higher self. It still comes from a false belief in wrongdoing. It means you felt 'entitled' to have someone meet *your* expectations, or share *your* needs and priorities, or obey the social rules, or be good and perfect in *your* eyes – even though that is not matching your vibrations! It means believing that someone can 'do' something to you that does not match your radio signals. Or that there can be any injustice. Or that anything can go wrong in a loving Universe.

Where there is unconditional love, there is no blame or guilt. Blame and guilt come from the world of judgment – and the inner voice of Love cannot see fault or wrongdoing. Love sees only innocence and goodness. As you reconnect deeply with Source, you come to a place where forgiveness no longer exists. A place of understanding, compassion and grace. A place where forgiveness is a nonsense, since there are no victims. A place where you remember that everything is governed by the law of attraction – that everything is a dance of co-creation. Now you're thinking like the Universe. And you smile to yourself.

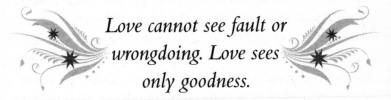

Love cannot see fault or wrongdoing. Love sees only goodness.

Handling conflict and difference

Conflict and difference are the main source of growth in relationships. Too much similarity or agreement is stultifying (which is why relationships often end if a couple is too much alike). But it's how you *handle* conflict that matters. If you are locked into fear-mode, you are likely to avoid disagreement. Conflict feels too threatening, so you tiptoe around difficult subjects and keep conversation to safe topics; in family therapy, this is known as 'ignoring the elephant in the room'. Or you might come up with win–lose solutions, in which one person's needs or opinions are seen as more important and valid, or one person feels entitled to control or manipulate another. (Parenting often falls into this trap – with parents either controlling their children, or sacrificing themselves – often while calling this love. Either way, it blocks us from *enjoying* our children.) Whenever you settle for win, lose or compromise – or simply avoid conflict – you are stuck in the world of fear, which spirals you into self-sabotage. It means that *everyone* loses in the long term, since growth and joy and expansion are blocked.

Relationships cannot function healthily from an unhealthy cosmology. Any thought of wrongness or fault or entitlement blocks open and honest communication – and means that the problem will not be resolved, but simply shelved for another day. If you want to be right, you cannot also be happy, since you are blocking the flow of Source. You have to aim for unconditional love for yourself *and* others. Healthy conflict resolution means having a no-fault agreement. No one can be in the right or in the wrong – even when it seems 'obvious' to you that they are! No one can be responsible for anyone else's feelings or experience. There is no blame, no guilt. No control, no sacrifice. No fight, no flight. No attack, no defence. No one needs to give in or compromise. No one is entitled to expect anyone else to behave in a certain way – whatever vows or promises they might have made. Everyone is treated with equal love and respect. When you see yourself *and* others through the eyes of Source, it pushes your consciousness beyond duality and into love-mode.

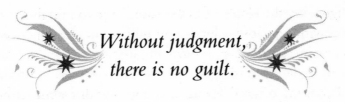

Without judgment,
there is no guilt.

To the Universe, everyone is in the right. They might have different values or needs or perspectives. They might be disconnected from Source at times, and acting from fear or judgment. But everyone is good and loving, and simply wants to be happy. And there is always a way of meeting *everyone's* needs. As you enter this larger reality – the expansive world of Love – it is amazing how often conflicts simply dissolve, or creative and unexpected solutions emerge from nowhere. You move beyond either-or, win-lose thinking into possibility thinking. Once you think like the Universe, you can always find a win-win solution for everyone. Not an unsatisfying or fear-based compromise, but a magnificent and fulfilling way through.

Love and freedom

When you get locked into fear-mode, it cripples romantic partnerships. Love becomes conditional, and is twisted into narrow roles and expectations – based on the needs for approval, control and security. You fall asleep, and repeat family-ar patterns of relating. This might feel safe, but it soon becomes dull and lifeless. It strangles everything that keeps love alive. It deadens romance, joy, passion, sexuality, sensuality, creativity, spontaneity, vitality and growth. You might cling to each other for security, companionship or social approval – or through habit, duty or convenience – but you are both imprisoned in a disappointing half-life. Conversation remains safe and superficial. You feel lonely even in each other's presence. Love is kept behind the glass walls of fear. You protect and defend yourself, or protect and defend the other. It is a pale imitation of real love. This is what many people grew up with, and so have come to expect of marriage or partnership. (And the law of attraction ensures you will surround yourself with others in similar relationships.) I call it 'tame love' – and it holds the soul in chains. Protection and denial build a dam that holds back the flow of Source energy.

Marriage has often conformed to this conventional dam-based model until now – a model that metaphysical writer Marianne Williamson described as 'a prison based on guilt and ownership'.[22] But love builds no prison walls. Love has nothing to do with protection, or with feelings of entitlement. Love makes no demands, and never asks you to pay a price. True love is unconditional. It is about a blissful communion of souls. It is about the miracle of discovering your individuality within oneness. It is about sensual embodiment and union. It is about reaching out and connecting, heart to heart. It allows you to reveal your truth and your darkness, knowing it will always be held softly in the light. In the absence of attack or defence – when we are fully present to one another – love arises naturally. After all, love is who we really are. And eventually, the flow of Love will have its way.

> *Love builds no prison walls.*
> *Love always sets us free.*

As our consciousness evolves, and our old patterns and defences break down – as our collective dam begins to trickle and burst – new models of relationships are emerging that break our old fear-based moulds. Relationships (of all kinds) that shake us out of our familiar habits and patterns. Relationships that melt our defences, instead of maintaining them. Relationships in which we can expand and fulfil our potential. Conscious partnerships based upon a deep intuitive connection, in which we fall more and more deeply in love over the years, while our love extends out freely and generously towards others. Relationships which awaken and inspire us.[23]

If you love someone without condition, you do not see their problems, weaknesses or limitations; you see only their strengths, their dreams and potential, and all that is wonderful in them. We all have both a clay-footed human and a golden angel within us – but Source, like our higher self, sees only the angel. Love is blind to what is bad or wrong. It sees only what is good and right. Love has unwavering faith in our highest potential, even when we are lost in fear or judgment, which is why a truly loving relationship – of any kind – brings out what is best in us. It sets us free to be who we really are. (Whereas conditional love brings out our feet of clay.) And as you raise your own vibrations or clarify your desires, so your relationships tend to shift – either growing with you, flowing into a different form, or flowing right out of your life.

Stagnation versus flow

When my friend Deborah unexpectedly fell in love, she was married with young children – and faced a classic and painful dilemma. Should she follow her heart, or stick to her marriage? She agonised over 'whether she had the right to choose her own happiness', despite the possible impact on other people. She worried about how it might affect their children. But she also wondered whether it was fair to stay with a man she did not truly love. And what about the impact on the man she did now love – who also loved her? After months of painful indecision, she trusted her feelings and left her marriage. Many years on, she is blissfully happy with her soul mate. Her husband soon fell deeply in love, remarried and had more children of his own, as well as taking on several step-children. Their joint children now have a large extended family and a hugely enriched life, with two happy parents and loving step-parents. Rather than a 'broken family' (a fear-mode term), it is a blended family that overflows with love. Deborah could have been dutiful, stayed in her companionable but lifeless marriage, and spent the rest of her life dreaming about what might have been – but how much joy, love and expansion they would all have missed!

In a cosmos based upon unconditional love, there are no wrong choices. No demand that you stick rigidly to commitments. No fixed paths or expectations. No cosmically approved lifestyles. No fingers pointing in blame or guilt. (All of that comes from fear.) There is only a finger pointing towards your desires. Towards your own heaven on earth. An evolving Universe supports flow rather than stagnation – which often means allowing relationships to flow into more appropriate forms if they have lost their joy and aliveness, or become restrictive and possessive. God is not an elderly, humourless and stuffy conservative in the sky, who favours duty and conformity – whatever the old religions might have us believe. God does not say 'You've made your bed and have to lie on it' or 'You must stick to the rules' or 'You must please other people'. That is religion serving as an agent of social control! God/Source is unconditional love. We are hardwired for bliss. We are designed for freedom and growth.

> *You cannot be responsible for anyone else's happiness. Only your own.*

As I see it, the current pattern of marital breakdown and re-marriage is part of our spiritual awakening. As a psychotherapist, I have witnessed how often dysfunctional family patterns are unconsciously passed down the generations. Children grow into adults who then mistake for love whatever they saw or received in childhood, and handle conflict and emotions in the same way. They often feel 'bound by loyalty' to similarly dysfunctional relationships in adulthood – and so the chain of pain is passed on. Until someone wakes up. Until someone reaches for Love. So perhaps the ability to let go of limiting relationships is essential in dissolving our fear-mode patterns, and giving the next generation fresh options and greater freedom? (If so, we need to stop judging a marriage as a failure if it ends in divorce. After all, some of the *least* successful relationships I know have lasted for decades!)

In an ever-evolving Universe, change and flow is constant. Nothing stands still. We are meant to be like flowing rivers, not fixed and unmoving like a mountain. If you resist change, life becomes more and more uncomfortable. Reality is designed to help you flow towards your never-ending desires. Everyone decides upon their own desires, and Source miraculously co-ordinates everything so that all preferences can be met – *as long as everyone follows their own flow.*

The Universe has limitless resources. It can make any choice the right choice. But if you are a round peg in a square hole, there will be painful slippage between you and You: between the stuck and limited mountain that you're expressing, and the fast-flowing river you really are. You will feel the discord, the divine discontent. And Source will be calling you, like a distant drumbeat, towards the You that you are longing to become. It calls you towards Love. It calls you towards freedom and growth.

Do you wish to be a stagnant pond – or a flowing river?

Freedom and selfishness

Freedom does not mean following every whim and fancy, regardless of the consequences – or being footloose and fancy free. As spiritual author Paulo Coelho puts it, freedom does not mean an absence of commitment; it means having the capacity to commit yourself to what is best *for you*.[24] Perhaps commitment is the wrong word, since this implies sticking with it 'no matter what' – with gritted teeth and joyless determination – rather than continuing to choose it, day after day, because it brings you so much happiness, growth and expansion. As soon as fear, guilt or duty become the motives for a commitment, resentment and conflict are inevitable; so are dishonesty and denial. *You cannot be true to another while betraying yourself.* Commitment must be an authentic and heart-centred choice. It cannot hold a guarantee, for life is always an on-going journey of discovery. Without freedom, intimacy is impossible.

Freedom means loving yourself enough to be true to yourself, and trust your emotional guidance. It means not giving in to what is socially expected, or what others demand of you, or what the inner voices of fear exhort you to do, nor feeling bound by past choices that are no longer serving you. It means making choices that express more of who you are. It means feeling your way into the flow. It means having faith in a loving cosmos.

If shifting from *being* good to *feeling* good sounds selfish or irresponsible – or it seems 'too good to be true' – you are not yet thinking like your higher self. You have not yet understood how emotional guidance works. You have not yet grasped that this loving Universe is carefully designed for selfishness. It is designed so that everyone can be happy, if only they follow their *own flow* (The only kind of 'selfishness' that backfires is expecting anyone else to change or limit *their* behaviour to make *you* happy).

When you see life as a gift, being true to yourself becomes a spiritual imperative – since what is best for the individual is always best for the whole. It took me a long time to fully grasp this, but it is a key to inner freedom. It means that you do not have to be good. It means that no one else can suffer if you follow your own dreams and desires (even if they protest from their fearful ego). On the contrary, it helps *everyone* to grow and change – to become more of who they are, to move beyond their old fears, patterns and defences. No one else can possibly pay a price for your happiness. And in a Universe based upon unconditional love, how could it be otherwise?

Since Source keeps everyone in mind, you simply have to go with your own flow. Until you realise that choosing to be happy is always best for *everyone* involved, you can be caught in neurotic conflict between fulfilling your own desires or pleasing others. Then you will keep attracting people into your life who make demands or feel entitled to control or guilt-trip you – until you set *yourself* free. Until you learn to follow your heart.

The truth is that anyone who really loves you will encourage you to follow your heart, rather than fit in and conform, or jump through hoops to please them – but sometimes you can only honour yourself by risking others' disapproval, or even rejection. By risking not being seen as good and perfect. Even by those you love.

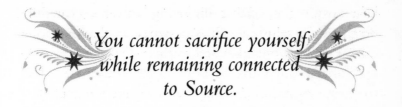

*You cannot sacrifice yourself
while remaining connected
to Source.*

Victoria arranged an urgent consultation with me last year. She was having panic attacks. Her father had suddenly announced that he was finding it hard to cope alone, and had decided to move in with her. Their relationship had always been fraught and ambivalent, but she felt duty-bound to give in. She couldn't see a way through. From her anxiety and despair, it was clear that Source was not calling her to live with her father. It was not a joyful choice, and would keep them both stuck in old patterns. But the Universe was mirroring her family-ar vibrations of guilt-tripping and martyrhood, and feeling responsible for others' happiness and well-being – unspoken family rules that had already led her to become a burnt-out social worker. The feeling that she had 'no choice' but to say yes to her demanding father showed she was reacting from fear-mode, rather than listening to the inner voice of Love. Whenever we feel trapped or disempowered, we are living from a fear-based mythology – and turning against the flow.

I reminded Victoria that Source never takes sides. It bears everyone in mind. Source always calls us towards happiness – and if we follow that call, the Universe can co-ordinate events and circumstances to suit everyone involved. If a choice makes you feel heavy or resistant, it is not serving either of you; it is coming from old habits of control and sacrifice. Habits based upon fear. And once you are fully in the flow, you sense this intuitively. After all, life is a gift – not a trial.

I urged Victoria to stabilise herself in love-mode before making a decision about where her father would live. Whenever you give in to guilt and demands, you are near the bottom of the emotional ladder – so the outcome will not be a happy one. A crucial psycho-energetic rule is that *whoever is more connected with Source dominates any interaction*. Since anger is a slightly higher vibration than guilt, someone who is critical or self-righteous can control anyone who is guilt-ridden or insecure – which is a common pattern in dysfunctional relationships.[25] It is therefore wise to avoid decision-making while you're feeling depressed, fearful, ashamed or inadequate, since any discussion is likely to spiral downwards, and the other person will wrap you round their little finger! On the other hand, if Victoria said no to her father while feeling bad about it, I warned her that he might become even more needy and miserable, mirroring her guilt-ridden vibrations. And unless she was in the flow, she would not be able to find the best alternative for him. She must come to peace with her own desire – by feeling her way into the flow – while asking the Universe to send the highest possible option for her father.

Several months later, Victoria wrote to say that her father was settled in a good nursing home, had 'chanced' to meet up with old army friends there, and seemed more cheerful than she could ever remember – and that she was moving towards a creative new career and, at long last, learning to love and nurture herself.

What is best for the individual is always best for the whole.

Finding your own path

The Universe would never have called upon Billy Elliot to abandon his dream of dancing, and follow his family down the mines; after all, it had given him his talent and enthusiasm. It would not have cheered if Deborah had given up the love of her life; after all, it had sent him to her as a gift. It would not have urged Victoria to invite her father to move in against her wishes; it had a far better option waiting in the wings. Harsh choices come from the old cosmology that suggests that love means sacrifice, that self-denial is virtuous, that you must fulfil others' expectations, that your feelings cannot be trusted, or that life is tough. Such choices come from living in fear-mode.

This loving cosmos never sends a desire that cannot be fulfilled. Nor does it challenge us to 'resist temptation', as the old religions would have us believe! The Universe is not designed to test or trick us. It simply wants us to be happy. It wants to deliver our gifts. It wants our fairy-tales to come true. And for everyone's sake, it wants us to merge with our higher self.

When someone has a mid-life crisis – perhaps abruptly leaving a marriage, job or lifestyle – it is usually because they have 'woken up' after years and years of fitting in, conforming and doing what others expect. Perhaps they have become ill or depressed, and suddenly realise why. They have been living a life that belongs to other people, and want to get back on track. On their *own* track. Even if they get lost for a while. Even if others disapprove. They are breaking free from their socially conditioned self, their tame self. Family and friends might see them as going crazy, but they are perhaps becoming sane for the first time in their lives.

In recent years, my own journey unexpectedly took me out of a marriage which had rocked me to sleep without my even noticing, and left me feeling small and diminished. The whole experience was tough and painful, yet it released so much that I had suppressed for years. It smashed through my old patterns and defences, and re-awakened my passion, creativity, dreams and sensuality. It changed me profoundly in ways that I could never have imagined. It restored me to myself, and taught me what love really means. I never had a moment's regret about my decision – and my ex-husband and I are much happier as friends and co-parents than we were as partners.

When you are on your path – when you are in harmony with your higher self – there is a deep sense of peace and rightness. Whenever you settle for a life that falls short of your dreams and desires, you will feel divine discontent. Something feels awry. It gnaws away at you. You are being called towards the heavenly life that you *could* create. If only you loved yourself unconditionally. If only you believed that life is a gift. If only you remembered that your dreams can come true. And until you do, the Universe is missing out on its evolution. And those whose lives you touch are missing out too.

*When you are on your path,
there is a deep sense of
peace and rightness.*

Love and self-love

Self-love is a prerequisite for loving others. You cannot love while you are in fear-mode, since you are turned in opposition to your higher self – in opposition to Love. You can be dependent from fear-mode. You can be dutiful or loyal. You can sacrifice yourself. You can play roles. You can even be controlling, possessive or manipulative. But you cannot truly love. From fear-mode, you are incapable of heart-centred love, emotional intimacy or authenticity. You cannot love with an open hand. You can only seek approval, control or security.

This is why it always backfires if you ask anyone else to conform to your demands and expectations – that is, if you offer conditional love. If you control someone through guilt or fear, they might give in to you; but you will pay a price. Whenever someone gives in, their higher potential is blocked. Sooner or later they will resent you and want to break free, as they begin to follow the healthy call of Source. (Ask almost any parent of a teenager. Or anyone who has felt controlled or guilt-tripped by a partner). Refusing to conform is often the first step towards self-love. It is the first step towards reconnecting with your higher self.

While you are trying to earn or deserve love, your vibrations are hovering around unworthiness and insecurity – and others will mirror that back to you. By the law of attraction, they will only give you as much love and respect as you give yourself. Despite what religion might have you believe, self-sacrifice comes from very low vibrations. It comes from a search for redemption. It does not come from Love. When you adapt yourself to suit others, you teach conditional love; and that is what you will receive. Once you value yourself enough to honour your own feelings and needs, and be true to yourself, you climb the emotional ladder. You reconnect with Source – and your relationships begin to shift.

Some relationships might no longer feel appropriate, as you remember who you really are, while others might grow and evolve. You become more colourful and multi-dimensional. You begin to spread your wings. Once Source is flowing freely through you, you become more and more loving. You have more and more to give. But you no longer sacrifice yourself for others; nor do you wish to control anyone. Your first priority is to keep your ego aligned with your higher self. You nurture yourself, and hold No one else responsible for your happiness. Inner conflict dissolves, and you are at peace. Then you can truly love – unconditionally.

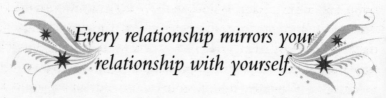

Every relationship mirrors your relationship with yourself.

Sticks and carrots

When you listen to the voices of fear and judgment, your motives tend to be sticks rather than carrots. You are driven by fear, guilt or insecurity. By duty and obligation. By following the rules. By trying to be good and worthy. By feeling responsible for other people's happiness. (As a friend joked to me recently, 'Oh, didn't you realise that I'm responsible for the happiness of the whole world?') Holding yourself responsible for anyone else's feelings is a sure way to drive yourself crazy. It not only imprisons you, but disempowers the other person. If anyone believes that their happiness or well-being depends upon your behaviour, it makes them vulnerable – so they try to control and manipulate you, so they can feel safe and comfortable. Then you are both stuck, and it feels oppressive and suffocating.

Just for the record, you are not here to please anyone else. You are not here to dance to the tune of others. If you try to do so, you lose your centre of gravity. If you make someone else happy *at your own expense*, you are not in the flow – and nor are they. No one else can be in touch with your emotional guidance. Unless you are loving towards yourself, you are not aligned with Source, and your actions will not be helpful. It is not your job to make anyone else feel happy. It is not even possible, since you cannot control anyone else's vibrations. (Nor is anyone else here to please you. If you believe that your happiness depends upon anyone else's behaviour – or upon the state of the world – you are giving your power away. That is conditional love). No one can be responsible for anyone else's happiness. And how anyone else behaves is none of your business. Happiness is always an inside job.

So how do you know whether a choice comes from fear-mode or love-mode? *By how it feels.* Always *feel* your way into a decision. If you make what you think is the good, safe or honourable choice (from your head), it is rarely what makes you feel happy and free (from your heart). Trying to think your way through means you might be misguided by others' needs or opinions or agendas, or by social or religious rules, or by weighing up the risks, or by avoiding rocking the boat – rather than being guided by Infinite Intelligence. (If you *must* think about a decision, just make a list of pros – instead of writing down the pros and cons – and see whether that clarifies the way forward. After all, the Universe never thinks in negative terms; it only sees the gifts.)

Always choose carrots, not sticks. If a choice feels heavy or dutiful, it is coming from fear. If it feels restrictive or inhibiting, it is coming from fear. If it feels virtuous or self-sacrificing, it is coming from fear. If it makes your solar plexus twinge or your heart sink, it is coming from fear. If it makes you feel smaller, it is coming from fear.

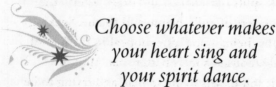 

Choose whatever makes your heart sing and your spirit dance.

In fear-mode, we are often governed by our inner judge or critic – which favours trial-like words such as discipline, willpower, self-control, duty, loyalty, sacrifice, 'should' and 'ought'. It admires self-sacrificing saints and self-punishing martyrs. It curls its lips in disdain over gift-like words such as self-indulgence, passion, sensuality, freedom, desire and imagination. It is deeply mistrustful of the good things in life. This denies our emotional guidance, and can lead to what I call an 'anorexic attitude' to life – based on self-denial, asceticism, avoidance of intimacy, over-achievement, hard work, perfectionism, ruthless self-discipline and heady over-control. It suppresses the divine feminine. It throws us into an inner civil war. (And it often goes with neuroticism over food and weight.) It leads to *being* good rather than *feeling* good – and so disconnecting from Source.

In a Universe based upon unconditional love, we are always and forever in a state of grace. We have no need for redemption, since we are blessed sparks of divine energy. Every part of us is good and worthy. There is no judgment, so there cannot be any sin, wrongdoing or imperfection. Our inner judge or critic constantly watches out for badness – but the idea of badness is the most toxic belief in life-is-a-trial mythology. It splits our energy, and drags us into the vibrational gutters of guilt, blame and shame. Seeking redemption by 'being good' does appeal to the fearful ego, since righteousness feels better than guilt or shame. But it still means living in fear, and trying to be ever-good and perfect. Once you reconnect with

continued ...

Love, you see that guilt and righteousness are both illusions. There are no wrong choices, paths, feelings or desires. And since every event is governed by the law of attraction, there are no victims.

It is only when you move beyond judgment that you leave the inner-outer battleground, and enter the heavenly state of grace. You move beyond the false duality of right and wrong. There is never any need for guilt, suffering, punishment or penance. You have no need to defend or justify yourself. Nor do you fear, attack or blame others. Your consciousness expands into the boundless world of unconditional Love. You see everyone (including yourself) as forever innocent and good. Then you can make choices which are aligned with your dreams and desires. You can become an embodied soul – and life becomes a joyous adventure.

*Until you live in a world
of grace, you cannot
be happy and free.*

The voice of Love always calls you towards your own heaven on earth. When you feel your way into the flow, your motives are life-affirming, joyful and heart-centred. You have no need to seek approval, keep yourself safe, or control others. You know that you are safe and loved. You are honest and authentic. You approve of yourself, whatever others might think. Once you are in the flow, indecision or confusion gives way to clarity. It becomes obvious what to do. You make choices based upon what feels good: passion, enthusiasm, freedom, creativity, expansion, reaching out with love. You make choices that make your heart sing. Choices which feel energising and joyful and playful, which make you leap around in delight. As your consciousness expands and you climb the emotional ladder, fear fades into the background – making way for a healthy ego and your higher self.

A healthy personality

A healthy ego (or personality) is essential. It gives you self-respect, clear boundaries, the ability to say no, awareness of your own thoughts and feelings, and a sense of individuality. It allows you to be uniquely you. It allows you to be fully present in the world. And crucially, it helps you to honour your own needs and desires. As soon as your ego has any desire, your higher self begins to hold the energy of that desire; it immediately *becomes* that future self. The only question now is whether you are going to join it – whether your ego can align with your higher self at an energy level – so that your dream comes true.

Your ego is not your enemy (though life-is-a-trial mythology would have you believe it is). Nor is anyone else your enemy. The nearest thing we have to an enemy is being in fear-mode. When your vibrations are low, the ego operates from fear-mode, leading you into defensiveness and self-sabotage. It is trying to ensure that you are safe and loved – but its only methods are fight, flight, freeze and addictions. It controls or sacrifices. It struggles. It feels like a victim or martyr. It is consumed by guilt or unworthiness. It looks out for threats. It squashes your feelings and desires. It is doing its best to help, but it keeps stabbing you in the foot. There is a painful gulf between your ego and your higher self. But as you climb the emotional ladder beyond anger and irritation, to hope and beyond, you shift into the healthy ego. You know that you are safe and loved. You reach for your dreams. You feel your way into the flow. You are true to yourself. A healthy ego (or personality) operates from love-mode, and works in partnership with your higher self.

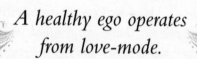

A healthy ego operates from love-mode.

Instead of listening to the clamouring voices of fear and judgment, or the heavy burden of social rules and expectations, quiet your mind – and listen for the inner voice of Love. It isn't as loud or insistent as the voice of fear, but it is always there in the background. It never beats you up with sticks; it only holds out carrots. It is calm and gentle. It is soothing and reassuring. It feels connecting and expansive. It feels light and liberating. It makes you feel secure and worthy and proud of yourself. It calls you into the flow. And it allows you to love yourself, others and the world unconditionally. Without anxiety, guilt or defensiveness. Without blame, attack or demands. Without needing anyone or anything to be 'perfect', or to adapt to suit you. When you listen to the voice of Love, your heart opens to the Universe. You behold the light and beauty within others, and your own dreams and visions expand. Like Ariadne's red thread, this voice can guide you out of the fearful labyrinth, and back into the light.

Now – what is *your* holy longing? Where is the inner voice of Love calling you?

Just for you

OWNING YOUR SHADOW

Which qualities do you most pride yourself on? Hard work and self-discipline? Moral righteousness? Spiritual awareness? Compassion for others? Being dutiful and loyal? Being kind and caring? Being rational and objective? Being solid and reliable? Being dreamy and intuitive? Being sensitive to others' needs? The more you pride yourself on any quality, the more their opposites will lie in your Shadow. (If you judge someone for being selfish or uncaring, you probably care too much for others at your own expense. If you judge someone for being lazy, you are probably driven and workaholic). Our strengths become our weaknesses, when we are out of balance.

What do you judge, despise or condemn in others (however subtly)? Is there anyone you tend to avoid, or see as threatening? Or anyone you admire, envy or long to be close to? Again, this gives you hints about what lies in your Shadow – your disowned selves, or hidden potential – the needs, qualities, strengths and desires that have been suppressed and are longing for expression, so that you become more balanced and whole. Unless you own whatever you see in others, these disowned selves will spurt out occasionally, or be projected on to others – or you will simply waste a lot of energy suppressing them, and failing to recognise their precious gifts. What do you need to express? Take back your power, and remind yourself that no one can 'do' anything to you. Refuse to see anyone as good or bad, right or wrong. Step beyond the world of duality – and feel your way into the flow.

THE INNER VOICE OF LOVE

Every time you hear yourself criticising yourself, others or the world, or seeing anything as bad or wrong, ask yourself, 'What would the voice of Love say?' Every time you beat yourself up for being imperfect, or fret over your life being less than wonderful, ask yourself, 'What would the voice of Love say?' Every time you give in to others' demands, or deny yourself what you want, remind yourself that love does not mean sacrifice – and ask what the voice of Love would say. How can you listen with an open heart, without fear or defensiveness? What if the Universe could meet everyone's needs and desires? How can you honour yourself in this situation? What is your holy longing? Every time you feel afraid or guilty or resentful, ask the voice of Love to speak to you. It is like exercising a muscle. The more often you connect with this loving inner voice – the voice of your higher self – the stronger it becomes. More and more, you will resonate with its energy, and see everyone and everything as a friend.

Chapter Five

Becoming a Laser Beam

You are like a radio station that can receive many stations.
What you receive depends on what you pay attention to.
Orin[26]

I recently watched the rapid rise to stardom of singer
Leona Lewis in a TV talent contest, and was struck by
how well she used some of the tools of reality creation.
She had daydreamed constantly about being a singer as a
child, then imagined her telephone headset at work to be
a radio mike while she entertained a huge crowd. By the
time she suddenly faced a live audience of millions – a

daunting prospect for any young performer – she was so well rehearsed at an energy level that she produced flawless, stunning performances. As one judge commented, she 'sang from her soul'. While she sang, her energy was totally coherent – every cell was dancing in love-mode – which made her charismatic and captivating on stage, and released the full power and potential of her voice. When she became ill with tonsillitis during the contest, she refused to beat herself up, soothed herself with the thought that everyone gets ill, and simply rehearsed the songs in her imagination (as she had done for years). While other contestants seemed overwhelmed by the sudden shift in vibrations required to deal with overnight fame, she had long been dreaming her way into that future self – and she shone like a beacon.

Visualisation is a powerful tool for reality creation. The cosmos will send you whatever matches your vibrations – so if you spend time each day happily daydreaming about your future, you magnetise it towards you. You might imagine a successful job interview, or walking hand in hand with your loved one, or running a marathon, or moving into your new home. The more real it feels, the more strongly you are attracting it. The Universe does not distinguish between a real and imagined experience; it simply responds to your vibrations. If you consistently hold the energy of a future self, then sooner or later, reality *has* to snap into place to match it.

*If you hold the energy of
a future self, reality
has to match it.*

Making your energy coherent

Have you ever wondered why a laser beam is so intensely powerful – how it produces light that can slice through metal? The secret of a laser beam is its highly coherent and focussed energy. That is, its light waves curve in the same direction at the same time, and work in synch – so they reinforce one another instead of cancelling each other out. They are also highly focussed on a small area. By contrast, the vast majority of energy emitted from a light bulb is wasted in destructive interference. For almost every light wave that curves upwards from the filament, another one curves downwards and cancels it out, while others dance off in all directions – so a light bulb is incredibly inefficient. Its energy is mostly inco-herent and diffuse. It isn't much brighter than a candle.

A laser beam says yes-yes, yes-yes, yes-yes, whereas a light bulb says yes-no, yes-no, yes-no or maybe this, maybe that – a form of self-sabotage. A light bulb is like a clumsy dancer doing a cha–cha – one step forward, one step back, step to the side – and wondering why it makes little progress. A laser beam is more like an athlete sprinting towards the finishing ribbon, never taking its eyes off the goal. If the energy of a light bulb were coherent, it would be thousands or even millions of times more powerful.[27]

The human energy system tends to mimic a light bulb rather than a laser beam. The radio signals that we send to the Universe on any topic often say yes–no, yes–no, yes–no. We dance back and forth, back and forth, between our desires and our resistance – between love-mode and fear-mode – like the push-me-pull-you creature in Doctor Dolittle. Our energy is split. Our higher self is saying yes and calling us towards it, but our fearful ego is saying no. So life remains much the same, even though we might consciously want it to change. Sometimes we even say yes–no–no, yes–no–no, yes–no–no – so things get even worse. For every step forwards, we take two steps backwards. ('Yes, I want this – but let me tell you how awful life is right now *and* how badly I have been treated.') Love-fear-fear. But if you can even say yes–yes–no, yes–yes–no, things will slowly begin to turn around. ('Yes, I want this and I trust I will get there – but I still doubt myself at times.') Love-love-fear.

If you can consistently say yes–yes–yes – deliberately holding yourself in love-mode – then reality will shapeshift in remarkable ways. You have become a laser beam, and are stepping towards your vast creative potential. The Universe can then send whatever you have asked for – sometimes with astonishing speed.

If you send yes-yes signals, the Universe can fulfil your desires.

Some people are naturally positive. If you grew up in a happy, loving family in which everyone's needs and emotions were honoured, with parents who adored you and wanted you to be happy rather than 'good', who saw life as a delicious gift, and believed that dreams can and do come true, then your thoughts will tend towards being laser beams. Your cells will function mostly in love-mode. You will be loving and accepting of yourself and others. You will trust your own feelings. You will feel safe and secure in the world. You will expect your desires to be fulfilled. The cosmos will drop gifts at your feet on a daily basis, and you will delight in every experience.

If your childhood was less than ideal – like most of the human race – you can still *become* a laser beam. You just have a little more work to do. You have to become more conscious and deliberate in your thoughts. You probably grew up with cha-cha habits of thinking, which make your energy incoherent – such as core beliefs that you have to earn or deserve love, that you are not safe, that you can be a victim, that you can make wrong or bad choices, that you cannot trust your emotions, that you must follow rules laid down by others, do your duty, or conform to others' expectations. Such beliefs will throw you into fear-mode at any hint of threat or disapproval, and disconnect you from Source.

If you grew up with control and manipulation, you become focussed on others' needs and pleasing them – so you lose touch with your own emotional guidance. 'Make me proud of you.' 'Don't cry.' 'Can't you eat that just for me?' 'Stop whining, or I'll give you a smack.' 'Be helpful.' 'Be a good girl/boy.' 'It will break my heart if you do that.' In other words, 'I will feel happy if you behave like this – so I want you to behave like this, rather than do what *you* want to do'. This is conditional love. Listening to messages like this means you lose yourself. You give your power away to others. You feel responsible for others' happiness. Then you fall asleep and forget who you really are. And you send out such mixed messages to the Universe that your dreams drift farther and farther from reach.

> *Seeking approval from others*
> *splits your energy.*

Getting into the flow

How do you know when your energy is incoherent? Firstly, you feel negative emotion or tension. This is guaranteed. It is your warning signal that energy is not flowing freely towards your desires. You are not in synch with yourself. You are holding thoughts that contradict the thoughts of your higher self, which is always in love-mode. Catch those thoughts – and turn them around! Secondly, you might feel tired or have physical symptoms of some kind – another alarm bell. Thirdly, you feel confused or ambivalent. You are unsure what you really want, or what direction to take, or feel torn between following your heart and doing what others expect. You waste a lot of energy trying to make decisions, and might remain stuck for months or years in a situation that feels unsatisfactory or painful. Your dreams will seem to be blocked, or you feel trapped and powerless – and the harder you try, the worse you feel. You are sabotaging your own desires. You have become a flickering light bulb, flickering between love and fear.

Let's suppose that a promotion is coming up at work, or you have seen a new job advertised – and you want it. How do you become a laser beam? Start by assessing whether you have any resistance to getting this job. If you can think about it and feel happy, excited and relaxed, with no trace of anxiety or doubt, then your energy is in alignment. You will feel confident, and the job is almost sure to come to you. If thinking about it brings up any tension in your solar plexus, that is resistance. It means that your energy is incoherent and split. The more hopeless or negative you feel, the greater your resistance – and the more inner work you have to do.

Listen to your thoughts about applying for this job. Perhaps you tell yourself that you don't have enough experience, or you're not good enough, or your boss doesn't like you, or you're bad at interviews, or so-and-so is bound to be offered the job, or someone else needs or deserves it more than you do. These are all cha-cha thoughts that contradict your desire. Remember that the Universe has already lined up the job for you. The moment you felt that surge of desire, the Universe said yes! Ask and it is given. The only uncertainty is whether you can send out yes-yes signals, rather than yes-no signals – that is, whether you can align your desire with your beliefs and expectations. Every time you take a step backwards, you will feel negative emotion to warn you that your energy is split. Any thought of anxiety, doubt or insecurity means you are sabotaging yourself. On the other hand, any thought of desire, faith, trust, confidence or even hopefulness will help make your energy more coherent.

Ask and it is given.
No exceptions.

Perhaps you have identified some negative thoughts and beliefs. Where do you go from there? Instead of seeing those thoughts as 'true', and even sharing your fears, doubts and negativity with others – which will reinforce them – you deliberately choose thoughts that make you feel better, which bring a sense of relief. You feel your way into the flow. You selectively remember times when your boss or others praised you. You remind yourself of others who were offered promotion despite their lack of experience. You make a list of all the reasons why this job would be perfect for you, and why you are perfect for it. You laugh softly at any thought that casts doubt on whether you might get this job – as if you were wrapping your arms around the Child within, loving and reassuring it. You keep reminding yourself to be a laser beam, which sends out nothing but positive signals about this opportunity.

You might wonder, 'What if someone else really wants this job too? How can the Universe say yes to us both?' The job will go to whoever is most aligned with Source. And if you are both aligned with Source, the Universe will find a miraculous way of meeting both your needs.

However, if you get caught up in feelings of competition – wanting to beat someone else, or not wanting to deprive someone else – that will split your energy. (Especially if you are English like me, since we are trained to be so polite and gracious!) It might help to say 'If I don't get this job, something even better will come along soon.' Or 'If this is the right job for me, it will come to me.' Tell yourself anything that helps you to relax. If a thought feels soothing or liberating, it is in the flow for you.

The Universe has unlimited resources. It can create wonderful jobs (or homes, or relationships, or prizes) for everyone! It expands in proportion to our desires. Whenever you believe in lack, scarcity or competition, you are disconnecting from Source energy. You are falling into fear. You are forgetting that this is a dream-like reality that you are creating – and you can have anything you want.

My friend Charlotte felt devastated when the house she had longed for was sold before she could free up her savings for the down-payment. After feeling crushed and despairing for a while, she reminded herself that everything works out perfectly, and that something even better must be on its way. She clarified what an even better house would be like. Sure enough, the perfect house came on the market within a few months – in a better location for her, at a lower price, and even with a mountain stream in the garden, which fulfilled a childhood dream of hers.

*Trust in the Universe. It knows
far more than you do.*

If you have held a dream for a long time, and it still hasn't happened, you can guarantee that you are doing the cha-cha. Your desire is not aligned with your beliefs and expectations. Or perhaps you keep noticing that it hasn't happened yet – which brings up doubt or mistrust or insecurity. You have to remind yourself that this is a loving Universe. You have to remember the law of attraction. You have to trust, to believe, to *know* that if you joyfully anticipate a dream coming true, then it will happen. It might not happen in the form you expect, or in quite the way you expect, or exactly when you expect it – but reality has to match your vibrations, sooner or later. (And if your vibrations are coherent, it will be sooner rather than later.)

Health and resistance

Does this mean that you could potentially overcome a genetic disorder, or restore a damaged body to wholeness? If you believe you can, potentially yes. Such miracles might sound unlikely or improbable – but this is a psycho-energetic reality. Energy can bend and twist into any shape or form you like. There are no limits other than those you believe in. The only immutable law is the law of attraction. Once Roger Bannister beat the four-minute mile, many runners soon followed in his tracks. He had broken through the *psychological* barrier of belief. In the same way, it is likely to take a well-authenticated case of someone reversing an inherited disease or re-growing an amputated limb before others believe it to be possible, and follow suit – but it is theoretically possible. We are now learning from the new biology, for example, that it is our *consciousness* that determines which genes are activated within our body.[28] In other words, we are not victims of our genetics. The physical body is designed for vibrant health and well-being, and it is only our energy-consciousness that can 'hold' it in a damaged or diseased state – as some doctors and scientists are now affirming.[29] Change your consciousness, and you change your health.

Believing that you are sick will hold your body in that pattern, and even exacerbate it, since we get what we focus upon. This is why a medical diagnosis can be so unhelpful. Deepak Chopra writes[30] about a friend who died of lung cancer within two months of a small tumour being discovered on his X-ray. After his death, an old X-ray turned up – and it showed that same shadow on his lung, five years earlier. It wasn't the lung cancer that killed him, but the diagnosis. (Or rather, how he *reacted* to the diagnosis.) Interestingly, the man had avoided seeing a doctor because he feared that a diagnosis of cancer would 'scare him to death'; and he was right.

Diagnosis can be helpful at times – for example, if you have been concerned, but the doctor reassures you this is a problem that can be easily remedied. But if you believe what 'experts' tell you, only consult a doctor who is relaxed and optimistic, and believes in your body's fantastic ability to heal itself – or at least is confident that their own bag of tricks will do the job!

Your body is designed for vibrant health and well-being.

The body is not a fixed and solid reality. It is a dynamic energy system. It mirrors your consciousness, and will perfectly mirror your self-image and your beliefs about health and ageing – as well as reflecting your current state of resistance. If your energy is mostly coherent, you are unlikely to have any health problems. If you tend to hover around frustration or irritation, at a medium level of resistance, you might suffer from minor problems such as headaches, indigestion, eczema or allergies. If you are resisting the flow more strongly, and often feel angry, critical, blaming or self-righteous, you might become vulnerable to ulcers, osteoarthritis, migraines, high blood pressure or heart palpitations. If you often feel guilt-ridden, ashamed, inadequate, trapped or despairing – or constantly focus on what is bad, wrong or dangerous – the battle energy within you eventually opens your body to life-threatening illness and serious auto-immune diseases such as cancer, strokes, lupus or coronary heart disease.

This is not an excuse to beat yourself up for becoming ill – to blame and shame yourself, and thereby make yourself worse. (Remember that blame always feels bad and disempowering, while responsibility feels positive and empowering.) For many people, illness and disease is a huge spur to their personal and spiritual growth. It is a heaven-sent opportunity for awareness and freedom. There is no incurable disease – though a life-threatening disease might simply be a way of 'choosing' to die (and there is nothing wrong with dying). But if you are ill and want to be well, the journey towards health and well-being is the same journey as making any dream come true: releasing resistance.

The underlying cause of illness is always vibrational – poor habits of thought, not trusting your emotional guidance, and being out of synch with who you really are. Becoming healthy is all about releasing resistance – soothing and reassuring yourself, loving yourself and life unconditionally, reaching for a positive future, feeling your way into the flow, and aligning your desires with your beliefs and expectations.

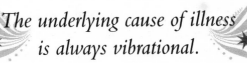

The underlying cause of illness is always vibrational.

Many people assume that a magical approach to life means that you should rule out allopathic medicine, which tends to ignore the psycho-energetic roots of illness, treats symptoms rather than causes, parts rather than wholes – and teaches us to look outwards to 'experts' for healing, instead of looking within. But there are no such rules, since everyone has their own unique emotional guidance. If you have a health problem, use whatever approaches give *you* a sense of relief, hope and optimism. The method matters far less than how it *feels* to you. If it feels good, use it! Modern medicine has a great deal to offer, and many doctors are true healers. But don't accept any treatment while telling yourself that it will harm you, since your body will react accordingly. Soothe and reassure yourself. Give your body positive messages, whatever your choice. And as far as possible, consult health practitioners who treat you respectfully as an equal instead of hiding behind a role, and make you feel nurtured, safe and confident about your body – and who empower you. That is, practitioners who are in love-mode rather than fear-mode.

Doing the cha-cha

You don't have to keep asking for what you want. The Universe heard you the first time. You simply have to stop doing the cha-cha. This means stop pushing against what you do not want – 'I don't want this illness, I don't want these debts, I don't want this painful relationship, I don't want war in the Middle East'– and instead focus on what you desire. It sounds simple and straightforward – and it feels good – yet it is not what we are used to doing! We are trained to focus on what is bad or wrong or lacking, what needs to be fixed, or how the world or other people need to change. We are used to dwelling on problems. But every time you moan or object or complain or even analyse What Is, you hold the vibration of What Is – and so attract more of the same. (And how do you know you are focussing on what you do *not* desire? Because it makes you feel bad.)

So how do you become a laser beam? Let go of your resistance. Stop building dams in your river. Stop dwelling on what is bad or wrong or lacking. Stop telling yourself why you cannot have what you want, feeling sorry for yourself, or getting others to agree with you about how awful it is. Stop analysing what is 'wrong' with you or others. Stop thinking about who is blocking your way, why someone else needs to change their behaviour, or whose fault it is. Stop justifying or explaining why you are so stuck or helpless or sick or poor – or why the current situation makes you feel bad. Stop talking about what you don't want. Stop blaming the past. Stop feeling like a victim. Stop giving your power away, and allow yourself to be an apprentice god/goddess.

> *Focus on what you desire.*
> *Focus on whatever*
> *makes you feel good.*

In other words, stop thinking about problems, and focus on solutions. Focus on where you want to go. Stop saying 'Yes, but…' – and just say yes. Focus on what you want the outcome to be – and keep your focus as pure and steady as a laser beam. Ignore anyone else's opinion or advice, however 'expert' or well-intentioned it might be, *unless it makes you feel good.* Avoid sharing your dreams with those who might cast doubts or shadows or judgment, unless you can shrug off their comments. Let go of any anxiety or doubt about the future. Whatever is happening right now, or occurred in the past, find a positive way of looking at it. Make peace with it. (Instead of beating yourself up for having a car accident, congratulate yourself on it being so minor, or having survived it. Instead of feeling self-pity over an abusive relationship, notice how it built your inner strength and self-awareness.) If any thought still gives you a twinge of tension, find another way of looking at it. This is the work of becoming a conscious reality creator.

Once you can think about an issue – such as money or relationships or health or work – and consistently feel happy, relaxed and confident, then what you want is on its way. The evidence might not be in physical reality yet, but that is just a matter of time. It is like a seed bursting into life below ground; you cannot see anything yet, but your *feelings* tell you whether it is growing healthily. Your emotions (which signal your vibrations) are your direct phone line to Source. According to Abraham[31], more than 99 per cent of any manifestation is complete before there is any physical evidence of it. So you have to keep on trusting and knowing. Don't fall back into doubt or discouragement (fear-mode). If you feel good when you think about it, it *is* on its way.

> *If you feel good when you think about it, your dream is on its way.*

Yearning and contradictory energy

One problem is that the more fervently you desire anything, the stronger your resistance tends to be. Why? Because any *strong* desire suggests that what you want is currently well beyond your vibrational reach. If it was within easy reach, you would simply desire it and expect it – and it would happen. No sweat. But when Source calls you towards a big dream that is covered in gold dust, and you catch a whiff of that future self and long to breathe it in, to become it, to dwell in that delicious life-changing reality – but also seriously doubt whether it is possible or even 'allowed' – then you throw yourself into conflict. This is the pain of resistance – it is the gulf between your ego (or personality) and your higher self. The gulf between your socially conditioned self, and who you really are. So now you have some work to do – to bring yourself into alignment with your higher self, so that your dream comes into physical reality.

It is often easier to create something you do not want desperately. A friend remembers gazing out of her window one winter, and wishing she had some seed for the wild birds. It was just a passing thought. Minutes later, a neighbour phoned who was packing to move house, wondering if she would like a large bag of bird seed. Ask and it is given! Instant manifesting often happens when we offer no resistance to a desire – or when our vibrations are very high. The more resistance there is, the longer we have to wait.

Yearning or desperation is always a sign of highly contradictory energy: huge desire combined with painful resistance. Huge desire with no resistance would lead to an exhilarating ride on the rapids – moving joyfully towards your dream, without a moment's fear or doubt. But any resistance leads to a roller-coaster of emotions as you swing from imagining what you want and why it will happen (saying yes to it) to worrying why it might not happen, or telling yourself it is unlikely, how it might upset others, or why you don't deserve it or should not even desire it (saying no to it). If this yo-yo becomes too agonising or exhausting, you might take the option of letting go of your desire with a sigh, and telling yourself it was an impossible dream; it was 'too good to be true'. Or you might carry on torturing yourself with the idea, without allowing yourself to move towards it. But nothing is too good to be true. This is a psycho-energetic reality, remember. It is not real and solid. You are dreaming your life into being. There are no impossible dreams – just sloppy or lazy creators of reality. Just people who have slipped into fear-mode.

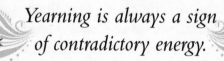

Yearning is always a sign of contradictory energy.

Instead of giving up on your dream, you can work to bring your beliefs and expectations into synch with your desire. This takes more effort than letting go of your desire, or pretending you didn't really want it, or keeping it at arm's length – but how much more satisfying and empowering it is! This is the joy of being a conscious co-creator with the cosmos. And the truth is that releasing a heartfelt desire always leaves you feeling empty and depleted. Once you have caught a whiff of that dream, there is no turning back. You might tell yourself you are being realistic or practical or responsible – but the truth is that you have betrayed your own soul. You will always secretly long for that dream. After all, the gift was yours for the taking. The Universe had already said yes. All you had to do was to step into that future self at an energy level. Instead you held on to your reasons for not having it. You stepped back into the world of fear and judgment – and became a flickering light bulb.

A recent client of mine had been trying to adopt a child for five years. As she sat down, she began a barrage of complaints about how inadequate her social workers had been, how bad and wrong the adoption system was, and how indefensible it was that she should be blocked like this from having a child. And (surprise, surprise) she knew lots of people who felt the same way! Since she had read my books, I had to press the Pause button to remind her that she created her own reality, and no one could stop her finding a child except her. Then she immediately launched into berating herself for doing *that,* and for all her 'issues', and why her dysfunctional childhood was to blame! I listened for a short while, then I had to giggle. Then we laughed together over the fact that her child-to-be might be waiting until she learnt to think more positively before coming into her life! Who wants a mother who moans and whines, and feels like a victim?!

Most of us can slip into this self-defeating pattern at times. (Certainly I can – and I teach this stuff!) Whenever we have a strong desire, we often develop well-practised habits of thought to explain why it isn't happening, and how wrong that is − and to gnaw over those thoughts again and again − instead of finding thoughts that feel good, thoughts that empower us, thoughts that will bring that desire into our reality. The stronger the desire, the more carefully you need to listen to your emotional guidance, since even a small amount of resistance will make you thoroughly miserable. *And* block your dream from coming true.

Focus on the positive

Whatever you desire, take no notice of what is realistic or true, *unless* it supports that desire. Reality is an ever-shifting kaleidoscope that is in your hands. You are moulding and shaping it like clay with every thought. Reality can come up with evidence to support any belief, since that is how the law of attraction works.

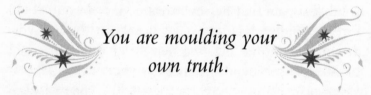

You are moulding your own truth.

The task of reality-creation is to focus on whatever aspects of 'the truth' support your dreams and desires − and ignore the rest. Or even make it up, and just *imagine* what you want. Let go of the past, unless you are milking it for happy memories that make your toes curl with pleasure. Sift through supportive snippets of conversation, or useful quotes from books. Do an internet search or watch films and documentaries about people who have achieved your goal, and use them as role models. Imagine how they feel. Tune into their vibrations. Make a collage of photos, news reports and images that remind you of your desire. Surround yourself with people who have fulfilled a similar dream. If you want a loving relationship, stop hanging out with couples who are miserable together or singles who bemoan their fate. If you want to be wealthy, avoid friends who whine about bills and debts and financial limitations – at least until you can listen while distancing yourself from their beliefs. Imagine you already have your dream. How do you think, feel and act differently now? Begin to hold the energy of your future self.

This might sound like burying your head in the sand, or being a Pollyanna, but this is exactly what will change your future. Nothing changes until you do. However, it does not mean *pretending* to be happy, and ignoring any negative emotion. Your thoughts and words have to match your vibrations (which is what it means to be authentic). Pretence and denial will never lead you towards your dreams. The Universe is never fooled by your lies or false smiles. It responds to the truth of your vibrations – to *how you feel*. You have to be constantly and sensitively attuned to how you feel, and be guided by your emotions to find thoughts, memories, conversations, situations and decisions that feel good.

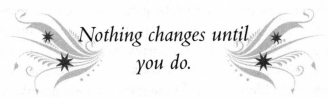

Nothing changes until you do.

Building your dreams

If a dream feels too far beyond your reach – if it just leaves you shaking your head in disbelief – then aim for something less challenging to start with. Don't aim for an overnight quantum leap in vibrations, or you are likely to fall flat on your face. Instead of conjuring up your dream home, how about a slightly larger house with a garden for now? Instead of the goal of writing a bestseller, how about getting your first article or poem published? Instead of attracting your soul mate, how about meeting a delightful companion for now, and seeing how it goes? Instead of aiming for perfect health if you are seriously ill, aim to be just a little fitter or more mobile each week. You will feel far less resistance, and move in the right direction.

If you can't think about a topic and find that crucial sense of relief – or joyful anticipation – there is an alternative. Focus your attention on something else. Something that makes you feel happy and appreciative. Something that helps Source energy to flow through you. Something that frees up your resistance. Whenever you feel blissfully happy, you are a laser beam. It doesn't matter what you are thinking about or doing, as long as you feel good. The Universe knows what you desire, and will send it to you as soon as it can sneak past your resistance; as soon as your vibrations are consistently high. You don't have to be a perfect laser beam. The Universe is not a hard task-master. Just send out more positive than negative signals. And it doesn't have to take long.

Within three days of deliberately choosing only

thoughts and activities that feel good, you will receive some sign or synchronicity that confirms you are moving in the right direction. Within three weeks, you can begin to turn your life around in dramatic ways.

What if you think, 'I can't be happy until I have this job/money/prize/achievement/relationship/home/ health that I want so much'? The paradox is that you cannot have it until you're happy as you are, since that desperate yearning keeps it away! As you keep affirming that you do not have it yet, it cannot come. As you focus on what is wrong or lacking, that is the radio signal you send out. The liberating truth is that you never feel awful because a dream has not yet come true – nor because anything bad has happened, or is happening right now. You only feel bad because you are going against the flow. And that resistance is what is blocking your dream, and making you feel bad.

You *can* be happy anyway. You *can* feel better without anything in your life changing. (And then it will change.) It is crucial to make peace with where you are right now. You are on your eternal journey. You are doing just fine. Stop doing battle with how life is. Lighten up and laugh about it. Then think about your desire in a way that makes you feel hopeful or optimistic; or focus on something else that makes you feel good. You just have to tip the

continued ...

balance in a positive direction. As soon as you
are going with the flow, the feeling of relief comes
immediately.

> *You never feel bad because a*
> *dream has not yet come true.*
> *You only feel bad because*
> *you are resisting the flow.*

If you cannot find positive thoughts about *that* subject, remind yourself of all that is wonderful in your life. Look at the beauty around you. Fill your life with simple pleasures. Meditate. Clear clutter from your house or office. Throw a clay pot. Grow vegetables. Paint a watercolour. Play the piano. Watch a comedy. Go jogging in the park. Stroke your dog. Phone someone who loves and appreciates you. Or pour your rage into a letter and then burn it, or scream into a pillow, or smash plates at a wall, if that makes you feel good. Do whatever it takes to get that blessed sensation of relief, of freedom, of relaxation, of being able to breathe easily again, which confirms that you are moving in the right direction.

You are now going with the flow. Don't turn back. Don't look behind you. Forget about the past. Don't get caught up in old habits of thoughts. Don't do the cha-cha. Throughout the day, keep asking yourself, 'Is that a resistant thought or a flowing thought for me right now? How does it feel?'.

Just keep going with the flow – and your dreams will soon flow into your reality.

Just for you

BECOMING A DAYDREAMER
Daydreaming helps to birth your future self. It is the ability to imagine what you want that makes you an active co-creator with Source. Imagine that you already have what you desire. Use all your senses to bring the scene alive. Feel it. Breathe it. Love it. Or just bask in happy memories that make you feel wonderful. Enjoy!

There are two secrets of visualisation. Firstly, get yourself into a happy space before you begin. If you try to visualise while yearning or in despair, it can leave you feeling even more hopeless. It splits your energy still further. So choose a time when you are feeling good – or start by relaxing, or conjuring up a happy memory, or sitting by an open fire, or sunbathing in the garden. (I do a lot of daydreaming in hot bubble baths.)

Secondly, just enjoy it. Sink into a happy daydream and enjoy the delicious feelings that it brings. If you daydream with the fixed intention of 'trying to make something happen', you are splitting your energy into What Is (which you are currently resisting) and What You Desire. By simply enjoying the daydream, you make your energy more coherent – and begin to vibrate in harmony with that future self.

MAKING A LASER LIST
Choose a desire to focus upon – and write down why you want it. (You don't have to justify your desire. The Universe has

already said yes! But focussing on 'why' can help you become a laser beam.) Now prepare a list of all the reasons why this dream is going to come true. Thoughts, beliefs and memories that support it. Affirmations that feel good. Helpful or positive comments from friends or family. Relevant examples from others' lives. Knowing that the Universe supports every desire you have. Anything that makes you feel 'Yes, this is going to happen!'

Different thoughts might feel soothing at different times, so write down everything that occurs to you. If any negative thoughts arise, write down positive responses to counteract them. Find ways of looking at the situation which make you feel better. Keep reminding yourself to be a laser beam. Keep your Laser List handy, so you can refer to it whenever you think about your desire and feel anything less than optimistic and joyful.

Chapter Six

Lighten Up and Let Go

At the level of the ego, we struggle to solve our problems.
Spirit sees that struggle is the problem.
Deepak Chopra[32]

Seventeen years ago, I took a leap of faith that changed my life. I resigned from my salaried post as a clinical psychologist so that I could write my first book, *Living Magically*. I had no publishing contract, and only the vaguest thoughts about how I would earn my living in future – but I trusted in a loving Universe. I followed my heart, and knew I would be guided step by step in the right direction. Before I had even completed my book, I received a request from former colleagues to run a workshop about my ideas. Through a series of 'coincidences', that workshop led to a guest appearance on a London radio station, which created a storm of interest – and within a few months, I had moved to London, was running increasingly popular *Living Magically* workshops, and had found my publisher.

Once you understand the law of attraction, and the nature of emotional guidance, you never need to struggle again. Struggle and efforting always mean that you are in resistance. As you relax, lighten up and let go, everything begins to flow. As you do what you love, you step into your higher self. Mythologist Joseph Campbell said, 'Follow your bliss… and doors will open.'[33] I have seen this happen on countless occasions. As you follow your bliss – doing whatever makes you feel good, nurturing yourself, appreciating yourself and others, filling your days with people you love, activities you enjoy and sensual delights – you resonate with the joy and well-being of the cosmos. And once you are aligned with universal forces, gifts and helpful coincidences are not far behind.

Does this mean you should resign tomorrow from a job that you hate? Definitely not. (I loved my job when I resigned; I had simply outgrown it.) If you are in a job you hate, you probably don't have another steady source of income, or you would already have left – so you might create even more problems by leaving it. Never move away from what you do not like; instead clarify and move towards what you want. Always shift your energy *before* taking action. Examine your beliefs about money and work. Set a clear intention to find a lifestyle that you truly love. Clarify what makes your heart sing. In the meantime, focus on whatever you appreciate about your current post, your colleagues, your workplace and all you have learnt and gained. You will find yourself relaxing into the job instead of resisting it – perhaps even enjoying it again – and that will open the door to new opportunities. Perhaps it will lead to travelling round the world for a year. Perhaps retraining for a new career. Perhaps setting up your own business. Or perhaps being headhunted by another organisation. And when that opportunity arrives, or inspiration comes, you will feel no doubt or anxiety. It will not feel like a courageous decision. It will seem inevitable and right – and every cell in your body will be dancing for joy.

Always align your energy before taking action.

You never need to worry about how or when something might happen. Just set your intention. The Universe can organise all the necessary events and circumstances, and in the perfect timing. Timing is all about aligning with your higher self. Avoid saying 'I want this to happen by next week, or next month', since setting a fixed time scale brings up resistance if part of you doesn't believe it can happen so quickly. You can throw yourself into conflict. (On the other hand, if it *feels* great, then go for it!) Likewise, you don't have to work out *how* to meet Mr or Ms Right, or how to find that ideal job or home, or how to pay off your debts, or find a creative outlet, or resolve a tricky issue. The Universe sorts out all the details of how and when and where. Don't try to hurry towards your goal, because the flow will take you there when everything is set up for you. If you hold yourself in vibrational harmony with any desire, the Universe *will* find a way to make it happen. It is guaranteed. That is how this magical reality works. Your task is simply to get into the flow.

Taking it easy

When synchronicities start to happen, that's a sign that you're getting in the flow. It might be switching on the radio and hearing the song that you were just humming to yourself. Or bumping into an old friend you haven't seen for years, soon after intending to track them down. Or overhearing a conversation about a trip to Egypt, just as you were hatching plans to visit the pyramids. Or perhaps you have your own signs that you are aligned with Source – such as a lucky number or symbol that pops up whenever the Universe is saying 'Yes, you're heading in the right direction'. (For me, the numbers 7 and 33 affirm that I am in the flow, or seeing rainbows, butterflies or tiny white feathers.)

Once you are in the flow – that is, you are feeling wonderful, and perhaps notice some synchronicities – you will feel prompted to take any action that is needed. You might feel an impulse to buy a newspaper, or pop into a travel agent or bookshop, or phone a former colleague, or sign up for a class in bird watching or photography. Trust that impulse!

While packing for a workshop in London recently, I felt a nudge to put two AA batteries in my bag. I shrugged, since I was not taking any electronic equipment – but I followed this inner prompt. While I was running the workshop, the radio mike for the PA system suddenly failed. Sure enough, it needed two AA batteries. I delved into my bag, and within two minutes, was able to continue speaking. When we are tapped into Infinite Intelligence, it is amazing what we intuitively know!

Any action that is aligned with the forces of the cosmos has the feel-good factor. It energises you. It feels liberating. It feels easy and right. Or it brings you relief. If it feels heavy, don't do it. Heaviness is resistance, a warning sign. When you feel as if you're wading through treacle, there is little point in taking action. You are not aligned with Source, and will be wasting your time and effort. Perhaps the timing is not right, or the action is unwise, or you have contradictory thoughts that need to be examined, or you are overriding other needs and desires. Whatever you do is likely to make things worse.

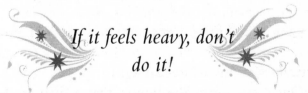

If it feels heavy, don't do it!

If you are striving to get a project finished on time, and ignore your desire to take a lunch break or accept a social invitation, that is when your computer is likely to crash, or you might have a car accident, or fall down the stairs and break a leg – mirroring your vibrations of feeling frustrated or overwhelmed. Efforting or pushing through resistance is always an act of self-sabotage. It means you are doing the cha-cha. Instead of pressing yourself even harder, devote some time to freeing up your resistance, and getting back in the flow. It will pay huge dividends. Before you make that potentially difficult phone call, focus your thoughts in a positive direction first, and set a clear intention for the outcome; don't pick up the phone until you feel good.

If you want to be a conscious co-creator, stay tuned into where you are on the emotional ladder (see chapter 3) and monitor the constant rises and falls. ('Hmm, I just dropped down to frustration on hearing that remark. How can I get myself moving up the rungs again?') If your energy is any lower than hope, or you notice a sudden dip in your vibrations, try to stop any activity until you have climbed up the ladder again – or at least feel a sense of relief. Taking action while you are out of the flow can be destructive, self-sabotaging or (at best) a waste of time.

In a psycho-energetic reality, the solution to any and every problem is vibrational. It lies in choosing different thoughts, which brings different emotions, which bring different realities. You are never vulnerable to what anyone else is doing, or 'how life is'. You don't have to change your circumstances or other people's behaviour, since what happens 'out there' will change once you shift your vibrations – or you will see it in a completely different light. And if there is any action you need to take, you will then be inspired to take it. You are the only person who can get in the way of your dreams coming true.

> *The solution to every problem lies in your vibrations.*

Finding your soul mate

If you try to meet a potential soul mate while feeling lonely and insecure, for example, you could spend every evening in night clubs and bars, surfing the internet or searching the personal ads without finding a suitable partner. Or you might meet someone who makes you feel lonely and insecure, or who affirms your negative beliefs. If you start any relationship while grieving over a past relationship, or while feeling betrayed or abandoned, you are setting yourself up for more grief and pain. If you expect a partner to 'make you happy', you are sure to be disappointed. A new partner will always match your current vibrations.

It is quite impossible to feel lonely when you are well-connected to Source — so get your energy flowing well *before* you move towards a possible new partner. Aim to feel happy, self-confident and in love with life. Live as you would live if you were madly in love. Treat yourself as you would if you were loved and adored. Become your own best friend. (This does take conscious and deliberate effort — choosing new thoughts, and feeling your way into the flow.) Align your ego with your higher self.

Once you are aligned with Source, you will meet Mr or Ms Right effortlessly. You will find yourself in the right place at the right time, or be guided towards the right action. You might feel that tingly sense of joyful anticipation, then bump into someone on the train, at a business conference or dinner party, or even through a wrong-number phone call. (Yes, I've heard of several people who met their husband or wife through a 'wrong-number' phone call.) Or you might suddenly 'notice' someone who has been in your social or work circle for years, and see them in a new light.

The Universe knows exactly where you and your potential partner are, and will guide you towards that meeting place – as long as you are going with the flow. And don't worry if you ignore an intuitive impulse, or feel tongue-tied in the presence of that hunky or beautiful stranger, and let them walk away. It is never your one-and-only chance. There will be plenty more opportunities.

I've lost count of how many 'miraculous' stories I've heard of people meeting their partner after using my *Attracting A Soulmate* tapes, which guide you to clarify what you want, release any resistance and become your future self. A British woman was surfing the internet while listening to my tapes when her American husband-to-be appeared on-line from across the Atlantic. Several people have reported meeting their future spouse while the tapes were still in the post, having set that clear intention! Releasing resistance doesn't have to be a big deal. You don't need years of therapy. (In fact, therapy can increase your resistance if it focuses on what is 'wrong' or what your issues are.) You don't have to work so hard at it. You can simply chill out, relax and trust – while the cosmos gets to work.

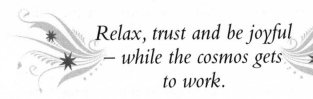

Relax, trust and be joyful
— while the cosmos gets
to work.

The power of letting go

A doctor I heard from wished to locate a business partner with complementary skills for a holistic health centre. He began a thorough and well-planned search for someone suitable using practitioner societies, telephone directories and the internet — then realised that he was efforting. It threatened to soak up his free time, and felt like drudgery. He trusted that his plans to find someone had sent a message out to the Universe. Then he sat back and waited. A few weeks later, he felt prompted to buy a health magazine — and found an article written by someone who matched all his requirements, had similar ideas and happened to live in a neighbouring town. Three years on, they have built up a thriving centre together.

The same take-it-easy principle applies to any creative project or desire. If I find myself struggling with a chapter while writing, I stroll down to the lake, or potter in the garden, or soak in a candlelit bath, or curl up in bed for a while. Taking a nap is far more efficient than efforting — as long as you don't feel guilty about it! It releases resistance. When I return to the computer, I invariably know what to say next — or I feel guided to work on another chapter, or shift to another project for a while. It feels easy, effortless and fun again.

There is a power in letting go, in surrendering. When we wrestle with any issue, our resistance often becomes entrenched. We turn around in circles, and dig a deeper hole where we are standing. Our negative thoughts become well practised and, by the law of attraction, attract more thoughts of a similar vibration. So whatever we want cannot come. As we let go and trust – not letting go of our desire, but handing it over to the Universe – our resistance melts. Which is why 'infertile' couples often conceive a baby after adopting a child.

If you have wanted something for a long time, and it still hasn't happened, try 'letting go and letting God'. Stop struggling to find a solution or a way through. Let it go. Forget about it. Make peace with What Is. Sometimes that is all that is needed – it is the final tweak – so that the Universe can deliver your gift.

> *You don't have to make it happen. You just have to let it happen.*

A fear-based cosmology will assure you that we only reap rewards through hard work, struggle and sacrifice. No pain, no gain. Or that you're only allowed to relax when you have thoroughly earned it, by grinding yourself into the ground. This is the secular version of the life-is-a-trial mythology, or the Puritan work ethic. But this comes from the limited world of fear, rather than the magical world of love and connectedness. The fear-based ego cannot comprehend how doing less might mean achieving more. It does not realise that shifting your energy and aligning with Source – and therefore emitting and receiving new radio signals – has far more impact than anything you *do*. When you expand towards your higher self, Infinite Intelligence is constantly on tap. You are far more efficient and productive. Time seems to expand and become limitless. It is like shifting from dial-up internet to broadband; everything flows more easily.

The Universe is designed to fulfil every desire that you might have – as long as you trust your inner guidance, and follow that emotional trail towards relief and joy and ease. So why do we keep efforting and going against the flow? Because we have been brainwashed into the old mythology of conditional love. Believing that we have to justify our existence. That we have to prove ourselves good and worthy. That we have to earn or deserve rewards. That we have to pay a price for happiness or success or money or even love. That we have to put others first. That suffering and guilt are somehow good for the soul. Many people were brought up to believe that self-sacrifice, martyrhood and over-responsibility for others somehow makes the world a better place. Or that having a hectic schedule and endless demands on your time affirms that you are important and needed. With beliefs like these, struggle can become a habit.

continued ...

'But you don't understand. I have all these commitments and responsibilities', you might argue. Have you really? Are they really as fixed and essential as you think? Would the earth stop revolving around the sun if that project was completed a week or two later, or the kitchen floor wasn't cleaned for three weeks, or you ignored your emails for a while, or said no to requests more often? Or are you being driven by a harsh, life-is-a-trial cosmology that tells you that you must work hard and stay busy? A mythology that will keep you out of the flow. (And if it is something you *choose* to do – such as paying the mortgage so that you can stay in the home you love, or studying for exams so that you can gain a qualification you want – then remind yourself of the bigger picture, instead of doing it while resenting your action.)

Efforting means you are going against the flow.

You *can* get results through hard work and persistence, especially if you have a clear focus – but you will waste a lot of time and energy. Whenever you are gritting your teeth, feeling under pressure, short of time or impatient, you are going against the flow. The truth is that the Universe is geared up to give you solutions, and shower you with gifts. Not because you have worked hard for them. Not because you deserve them. Not because you are worthy of them. (Your worthiness is never in question.) Simply because you have asked – and the Universe has said yes.

Opening to receive

Notice how you deal with compliments or free gifts, and it will reveal a lot about your cosmology. Do you shrug it off or deny it when a friend says you look wonderful, or your boss congratulates you on recent work? Do you silently tell yourself they are mistaken, or just being kind? Perhaps you immediately return the compliment, in order to 'pay' for it? Or do you simply accept with a warm glow of appreciation? How do you accept an unexpected gift or offer of help from a friend? How do you respond when someone says they love you? You probably respond in the same way to the gifts of the cosmos. Sending them away. Paying for them. Or simply saying yes – with gratitude and appreciation.

Receiving *is* your gift to the Universe. That is what helps the cosmos to expand. Isn't that an amazing thought? The Universe is evolving (in part) *through you*. You dream and desire. The Universe says yes. You accept your gifts. Then the world changes and grows. Saying no to your gifts helps no one. Staying stuck or avoiding change helps no one. No one benefits through your suffering and martyrhood. No one else becomes more prosperous because you have less money. No one else becomes more healthy if you remain ill. The cosmos has unlimited resources. It expands in proportion to our dreams and desires and beliefs and expectations.

As we collectively desire, imagine and expect sources of energy that are cheap, renewable and abundant, so it will be. As we collectively desire, imagine and expect cheap, safe and effective health care, so it will be. As we collectively desire, imagine and expect non-polluting cars and trains and planes, so it will be. This is not a fixed, solid reality. We are dreaming the world into being. This is a psycho-energetic reality – limited only by our imagination, and our willingness to receive.

Open to receive gifts, instead of striving to earn rewards.

Does this mean that you don't have to do anything? Just sit back and dream, peel a few grapes and wait for your gifts? On the contrary, you are here to revel in being alive! To fill your days with wondrous experiences and stimulating conversations and loving relationships and sensual pleasures. To create the lifestyle of your dreams. To follow any joyful impulses, and throw yourself passionately into projects that feel exciting or visionary. To contribute to the world in whatever way feels delightful and inspiring to you. Open yourself fully to life and love. But what you don't have to do is stay in control. You can surrender that to the Universe. Trying to control usually means you are going against the flow – so you are moving away from what you want. You might feel tense or agitated or worried or critical or angry or tired or bored or disempowered. Your traffic lights are on red. Then it is time to relax, take a deep breath and remind yourself that the Universe is in charge. All is well. Just envision what you want – then let it unfold. Chill out. Lighten up. And yes, perhaps even peel a few grapes.

LETTING GO OF CONTROL

Have you ever noticed that those who diet or count calories tend to be overweight – while those who never worry about their weight tend to stay slim while eating whatever they fancy? It isn't that slim people are 'lucky' enough to have a fast metabolism; it is that they trust the body instead of going into battle against it. The more you try to control anything (or anyone), the more out of control you tend to feel – because trying to control comes from lack of trust and faith. It comes from fear and disconnection. It always backfires on you. The body is designed to maintain a healthy weight, if only you stop sending it 'Oh my God, this will make me fat' messages, which your body feels obliged to confirm! We get what we focus upon. Focus on a weight problem, and that is what you will have. Instead throw out your scales, trust your body, and picture yourself at your ideal weight. Or ask yourself whether you *want* to fit in with social pressures to be slim, if you are naturally plump or curvaceous.

Life-is-a-trial mythology can fill us with fear and judgment about food. It suggests we cannot trust the body or our desires. It warns us about the dangers of 'unhealthy' or 'fattening' food. It sends us into battle against ourselves, and sees self-denial as virtuous. No wonder so many people have eating disorders or weight problems! When you shift into the life-is-a-gift philosophy, you relax and let what you eat be guided from *within you* – by your natural and healthy appetite – not by diet books, calorie charts or the latest food fads and theories. You stop splitting food into good (healthy) and bad (junk) food, since it splits your energy whenever you eat anything you label as 'bad', or force yourself to eat something because it is 'good for you'. You trust your body to stay healthy, and to give you any messages you need. And you no longer try to block your emotional guidance by stuffing your feelings down with food. You just eat whatever feels good to you, and *enjoy* it. You stop making it such a big deal. Your body is unique, and is always your friend – and so is food – as long as you stop treating it like an enemy.

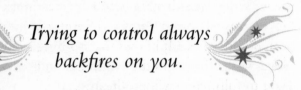

Trying to control always
backfires on you.

In the same way, you can trust the Universe to take care of you, to know what you desire – and to find a hundred possible ways of delivering your gifts. It *wants* you to be deliriously happy. It has your best interests at heart. All you have to do is let go of your resistance. Relax, lighten up – and let go.

Balancing the cosmic scales

I often see life as a pair of cosmic scales, with your everyday you on one side and your higher self – the You that you are becoming – on the other side. When you think like your higher self, the scales are balanced and you feel fabulous. Your life feels in balance. You are in the flow. Everything you desire comes to you easily. When your thoughts are heavier than those of your higher self – when you weigh yourself down with fear or judgment – your scales tip out of balance. You feel heavy, disempowered, trapped, uneasy or agitated. You might be beating yourself up, or blaming someone else, or regretting the past, or feeling hopeless and stuck, or railing against What Is. You are not listening to the inner voice of Love. Those heavy or uncomfortable feelings are the painful gap between you and your higher self. You are not thinking like the Universe – which sees you as a powerful co-creator, a passionate dream-weaver, surrounded by other wondrous beings in a magical and joyous reality that is forever unfolding. It knows that you can do no wrong. It knows that nothing can go wrong. It loves you, others and the world unconditionally. It wants you to fulfil your wildest dreams.

> *Your higher self is always proud of you. Always.*

Even when life is challenging, and you're sitting like an elephant on your end of the scales, you can choose to lighten up and let go. As soon as you are just moving in the right direction – by choosing new thoughts or making new decisions – you feel that oh-so-delicious sense of relief. Your higher self is now saying, 'Yes, yes, keep going, love yourself, be happy, take it easy, believe in your dreams. Your gifts are waiting for you. Come this way! Come this way!' Angels fly because they take themselves lightly – so give up the struggle. Let go of control. Have faith and trust. Practise saying 'No big deal'. Laugh often. Follow your bliss – and doors will open.

Just for you

RECEIVING GIFTS

Notice how you react when a friend or your boss gives you a compliment, or gives you a bonus or gift, or offers to pay for a meal. Do you automatically return the compliment, whether or not you mean it? Do you feel awkward or reject it? ('Oh no, I look awful.' 'I've had this outfit for years.' 'No, you can't possibly pay for that.') Do you give them a hard time, or refuse to accept any gift without paying them back? Or do you accept easily and graciously? Do you feel worthy of gifts? Are you open to receiving? Can you accept gifts from the Universe?

LIGHTENING UP

If a project or situation feels heavy or burdensome or stuck, find some way of lightening up. Take a break. Have a massage. Buy some candy floss. Blow bubbles in the park. Meet a friend who makes you laugh. Ask yourself whether you are making heavy work of this – instead of just using the law of attraction, and allowing your desire to come to you. Think about ways in which this problem could be nightmarishly worse than it is, until you make yourself giggle and relax. See yourself sitting on the moon, gazing down at this strange creature who is getting stressed over such a minor project or concern. Picture yourself five years on, and realise how trivial or forgettable it will seem by then – or at least well behind you. Clear yourself of old energy by de-cluttering a kitchen cupboard, or taking your old clothes to a charity shop. Put on a red clown's nose, stare at yourself in the mirror – and laugh.

Chapter Seven

Everything is Unfolding Perfectly

The silver lining is always as bright as the cloud is dark.
John F Demartini[34]

If you expect life to be perfect, you've probably come to the wrong planet – or even the wrong cosmos. Life could only be perfect if it were stagnant – like the mythical afterlife in which angels flap around and play harps, and all the human souls rest in eternal peace. Yuck! Imagine how yawningly dull that would be. Who would want to be seen dead in such a place?!

Creating heaven on earth doesn't mean making life perfect, then giving up and going home, mission accomplished. Nor is life about becoming good and perfect yourself (which would imply there is something bad or wrong with you). Creating your own heaven on earth is about clarifying what you want, then focussing your energy – or at least keeping out of your own way – so that you create it. By the time you have created that, you will have fresh new desires, and off you go again. In the meantime, you enjoy life as it is right now – even though it isn't yet all that it might be. You know that it never will be complete, because life is a journey not a destination, so you learn to enjoy every step along the way. This is the joy of being an apprentice god/goddess – and if you can create consciously and deliberately, it is so much more fun!

You are an eternal being in conscious evolution, and your journey will never end. You have free will to choose your own path, day by day – and you cannot get it wrong. No matter what you are facing right now, everything is unfolding perfectly. In fact, the worse it gets, the more glorious the future that awaits you, as long as you can get out of your own way. However messy and chaotic your life appears to be, the Universe is beautifully designed to lead you towards your dreams and desires – often in unexpected ways. You might have a collapsing roof, or crippling debts, or a pending court case, or your partner might have just walked out on you. You might have been made redundant, or slipped a disc, or found a herd of cows in your prize-winning garden. Yes, you have created whatever you experience. Yet nothing is ever going wrong. There are no wrong paths. There are no wrong choices. No one up there is awarding gold stars or black marks. There will be no Judgment Day. You have no need – ever – for guilt or regret. And you can always get to where you want to be from where you are. Always. (Your higher self already knows this. I'm just reminding you.)

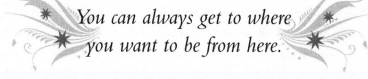

You can always get to where you want to be from here.

The gifts of contrast

This is a perfectly imperfect Universe. So the bad news is that you often have to crash and bang into experiences you don't like in order to clarify what you do like. If you were 'perfectly' happy and content, you would have no desires and preferences – so nothing would change. Contrast, variety and difference are essential to the birth of fresh desire, which is the basic building block of this ever-expanding Universe. The cosmos cannot deliver gifts unless you keep asking for new gifts. And it wants you to keep asking, since that is how consciousness evolves! So you need to experience what you do not want at times, so that you can make fresh choices and give birth to fresh preferences and choices. Contrast is the gap between What Is and your current personal or global dreams. Contrast is the grain in an oyster shell that yields a precious pearl. It is the irritation that stimulates a desire for growth and change. And the greater the irritation, the larger the pearl.[35]

Why would anyone choose to experience an abusive childhood, or poverty, or homelessness, or bankruptcy, or an unhappy marriage, or physical disability, or a scary diagnosis? It might seem crazy from our limited personality's perspective – but from a bigger perspective, we know that such experiences make us yearn for life to be different. They make us long for loving relationships, for prosperity, for a healthy body, for freedom and joy and ease. Pain comes from feeling separate from Love.

When we feel disconnected from Source, we long to reconnect. And that fervent longing is the springboard that launches us towards a bright new future. A future your higher self has already created, and is calling you towards. Nothing is ever created without being desired and imagined first – and how you yearn for freedom when you feel trapped or imprisoned. How much you ache for love and intimacy when you are controlled, criticised or kept at a distance. How much you wish for a stable home or financial security when you are thrown out by bailiffs, your business fails or your debts spiral. How you long for inspiring and heart-centred work when you are in a dull, repetitive or meaningless job. How you yearn for health when given a worrying diagnosis. Deep down, you know that life is not meant to be like this. Life is meant to be wonderful. Contrast wakes you up, and stops you being sleepy and complacent. It throws you into the crucible of change – which is why, in this age of awakening, many of us are going through exaggerated contrast right now.

The greater the irritation, the larger the pearl.

This is what is meant by the old saying 'Suffering is good for the soul'. Suffering is *not* good for the soul – but it can lead you to reach for joy, to reach for your dreams, to move towards your higher self. It might give you invaluable experience and insights about love, self-empowerment, trusting in the Universe, being true to yourself and so much more. Once you have delved into the depths of grief, pain, terror or suicidal despair, you have been there and survived – so there is nothing to fear any more. It becomes easier to remain present in love when faced with conflict or challenge, instead of becoming defensive and retreating into fear-mode. If you have been through tough times, you know how trans-formative they can be – as long as you shift to a higher perspective, and begin to look for the blessings. Then focus on where you are going. Focus on closing the gap between your personality and your higher self.

The danger is that you can get snagged on the thorns, and forget to look for the roses. Then you might repeat the same experiences over and over – like the woman who gets involved in one abusive relationship after another, or the man who gives up an addiction to alcohol only to become addicted to work, gambling or exercise. Or when you cure one illness only to fall ill with another disease. Or become a therapy junkie, endlessly recycling your childhood in a vain attempt to free yourself of it.

Unless you learn to smell the roses – using painful contrast to clarify your desires, expand your awareness and shift your vibrations – nothing is going to change. The Universe will keep guiding you in the right direction emotion-ally, but you might cling to self-pity and victimhood, blaming other people, feeling imprisoned by past decisions or current circumstances, or repeating old patterns of thought and behaviour – so you keep attracting the same experiences.

Contrast is not an excuse to beat yourself up. Nor is it a badge of honour to wear with pride. ('Look how much I've suffered!') Contrast is simply inevitable in an evolving cosmos. Life will never be exactly as you want it to be (or not for long). Not because you are being sent lessons. Not because you have messed up as a reality creator. Just because change and evolution is a constant of life – and if life remains the same, your growth comes to a halt.

In this current age of spiritual awakening, many people are going through extraordinary challenges and great darkness, since extreme contrast can lead to quantum leaps in consciousness. The deeper the contrast, the greater the potential for growth. There are no mistakes. Every difficult or painful experience is full of opportunity – if only you look through the eyes of love, rather than through the eyes of fear or judgment.

> *Contrast is essential in an evolving Universe. It gives birth to clarity and desire.*

I recently went through two years of intense and irresolvable grief over being separated from a man I loved – unable even to see or speak to him, though he lived nearby. No one could have been more present in his absence, since he was someone I loved unconditionally, for the first time in my life. An ancient and boundless soul love. I caught only fleeting glimpses of happiness throughout this crazy-making period. Those involved acted like caricatures of the different creation myths – mirroring battling aspects of myself – while I floundered in-between, looking for a healthy and open resolution, while trying to honour others' needs. I realised how much of my life I had strived to be good and perfect, and how often I had held back instead of being authentic. It is not an experience I would ever wish to repeat, but it was the most transformative journey of my life.[36]

In retrospect, I could have avoided much of that pain – if I had stopped judging myself, giving in to others, analysing what was wrong, feeling such a strong sense of injustice and 'pushing against' the situation. Or if our relationship had mattered less to me. But would I have learnt so much, had I not been so deeply motivated to move through the gruelling pain and reconnect with Love? Would my heart have opened so much? Would I have become so sensitive to my own emotional guidance? Or launched such vivid personal and global desires for loving relationships and honest communication? Would I have found out *why* being good and perfect does not make us happy? Or understood the close links between reality creation and unconditional love? Would I have finally learnt that my happiness does not depend upon other people or circumstances? Would my faith and trust in a loving cosmos have become as deep as the ocean? I doubt it.

When I finally emerged from that dark and confining

chrysalis, I felt like a different person. A butterfly with damp, unfurling wings. I felt astonishingly awake and alive – and was profoundly grateful for it all. Sometimes we have to be willing to dive into the deepest darkness in order to reclaim who we are. As the poet Rilke said, 'I have faith in nights.'[37]

Transformation is often borne of chaos and upset, a shaking-up of the old order. At such times, life can take on a mythic quality as we become heroes and heroines in our own epic journey – and often we only see the blessings when we have moved through the situation, since pain and grief blunt our consciousness. As poet and philosopher John O'Donohue puts it, 'The light that suffering brings is always a gift that it leaves as it departs.'[38] But you can trust that the gifts will unfold in their own time – like a rainbow after the storm.

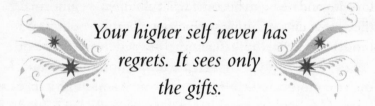

Your higher self never has regrets. It sees only the gifts.

Everything changes

As parents, many of us want to protect our children from contrast – to avoid situations that might ruffle their feathers, challenges they might not be ready to handle or people who might bruise them, or to make them feel safe and secure by avoiding change. But change and variety is essential to our growth. And the more we trust in a safe and loving Universe, the more our children will do the same – and emit those vibrations of love and trust and empowerment, instead of seeing the world as a dangerous place. Children pay far less attention to what we say than to how we feel and behave. Children cannot be fooled by pretence; they are highly attuned to vibrations.

Most parents believe they must teach and guide their children, but the truth is we should be learning from them. When they feel controlled or disempowered, they feel healthy anger. Children are far less resistant than adults, far more authentic and trusting of their emotions – more naturally in the flow – until we teach them otherwise. Until we teach them to conform and please others. Or teach them to be fearful or defensive.

If the high and coherent vibrations of unconditional love, joy and freedom become what children see as normal, they grow up resonating with those vibrations. But if you model fear, blame, guilt, shame, self-sacrifice, avoidance or denial, those are the energy patterns your children pick up. The more you tackle your own problems with inner strength, confidence and love – changing *yourself* instead of shrinking back, avoiding conflict, giving in, protecting yourself or blaming others – the more you become a positive role model for your children.

As you expand into your higher self, you realise that contrast and variety is not something to avoid. It is something to embrace, so that it yields its pearls. Which is exactly why a loving God/Source allows us to experience pain and distress. Like a loving parent, the Universe trusts that we are invincible. We are resourceful. We can handle it – and reap the rewards. The more you think like the Universe – which means seeing the bigger picture, and moving towards your higher self – the less resistance you feel towards any contrast. You do not judge any experience as bad. Everything is perfect in its own way. You love life unconditionally, and simply use contrast to fuel your visions for the future. ('Ah, this is what I'm currently attracting – but *this* is what I really want. *This* is where I am going.') Facing problems makes us go within, or reach for creative solutions – which expands our consciousness. Whatever happens, all is well.

One tool for releasing resistance to contrast is to remind yourself that this is 'just for now'. It is temporary. However overwhelming your pain, hurt, anger, grief or frustration might seem right now, it will pass. Everything moves on. And how long it takes to change is not dependent upon luck or chance, or anyone else's decisions, or the usual length of the grief process, or how faulty the legal system or government is, or whether someone realises how 'badly' they are behaving! How long it takes to change is entirely up to you. Your thoughts. Your beliefs. Your vibrations.

This situation (or this pain) is only temporary; it will pass.

Even if it seems to be a fixed situation – such as a bereavement or physical disability – you can still change your *perception* of it. I remember the mother of a blind child who told me that my books had helped her shift from the pain of seeing her son as disabled and faulty to seeing him as different and unique. She realised that he had chosen this, at a soul level, for the gifts it would bring. She stopped feeling like a martyr, and her grief and frustration slowly turned to pride. If the situation cannot change, you can always change how you think about it. And *that* changes everything.

Sunny Side Up

So how can you handle contrast in positive ways, so that you minimise its pain and maximise its benefits? How can you close the gap between What Is and what you desire? How can you hold to the reassuring awareness that – however bad it might look – everything is always unfolding perfectly?

A crucial skill in dealing with any challenge – as a conscious co-creator – is flipping to its light side. There is always a dark and a light side. All you have to do is focus on the light. I call this the Sunny Side Up process. Let's suppose your car has just broken down for the third time in a month. You can focus on how useless and unreliable the car is, how you cannot afford to replace it, how expensive the repair bill is likely to be, how hopeless the garage is that had apparently fixed it, or how you always seem to buy rotten cars. Moan, moan, moan. Whine, whine, whine. Thinking like a victim. You might even remind yourself that you create your own reality, and use that to beat yourself up. 'Stupid me for creating this! Why can't I get anything right? Why didn't I get the message and sell this car before it cost me a fortune?' Shaming yourself. Guilt-tripping yourself. Telling yourself how faulty and inadequate you are. *Not* very helpful! This is dwelling on the dark side – and it keeps you stuck in the mire.

If you think Sunny Side Up, you shift rapidly to focussing on what you want – and to gratitude. You might use this breakdown to clarify that you want a car that is reliable and cost-effective, and begin to imagine what that new car will look like, and how it will feel to own it and drive it. You can feel your way into that future self. You might appreciate the experience for sharpening your focus, and making you aware of negative thoughts about cars, money or other issues. Perhaps it mirrors thoughts about people in your life being unreliable? Or maybe it mirrors frustration or irritation (which are both signs of feeling disempowered)? Or you might realise that the breakdown prevented you doing something that you didn't really want to do. Or was it serving you in some other way? What are the blessings in this situation? You might also appreciate how quickly a recovery truck arrived, or the caring angel who offered you a lift. And you might be grateful that you have a car at all, and that it works most of the time! Instead of focussing on what is bad or wrong – which will bring yet more breakdowns, or another unreliable car – you focus on the positive.

You don't have to face an emergency before you use the Sunny Side Up process. If you get the hang of using it on a daily basis, you will slip into it automatically in a crisis – instead of going into fight-flight, and turning what could be a minor blip into a full-blown catastrophe. Turning Sunny Side Up comes naturally to optimists, who focus on the best and soothe themselves constantly. As a conscious reality creator, you need to be sensitive to your vibrations above all else, and immediately ask what triggered even the slightest dip in your emotional state – then either find a thought that brings relief, or flip from a negative to a positive focus. If you catch it early, this can stop you spiralling into a nose-dive in the face of a critical comment, tragic newsflash, broken window or lost contact lens.

 You are safe. You are loved. All is well.

Last year, I ran out of petrol en route to a workshop I was attending. Instead of criticising myself for ignoring the fuel gauge, or worrying that I might disrupt the workshop and what I would miss, or analysing why I had created this – as I might have done in the past – I quickly turned Sunny Side Up. I focussed on my desire. I was a long way from home, and since I don't belong to a breakdown recovery club, I needed help from strangers. And I wanted fuel – and quickly. I sent out my request to the Universe, and kept a positive focus. It would all work out perfectly. Within five minutes, a white van pulled up behind me, and four burly men announced they were from the Highway Patrol Agency. My angels had arrived! They gave me a free lift to the nearest service station, then topped up my tank for me – and I was only a few minutes late for the workshop. If I had slipped into worry, self-pity or shame, I'm sure I would not have magnetised such efficient help.

Thinking like the Universe

When you think like the Universe, it can help you through the deepest and darkest of contrast. A couple of friends visited recently who had lost almost everything they owned. On the previous weekend, sparks from a wood-burning stove caused a devastating fire which swept through their wooden cabin, destroying all their clothes, books, furniture and belongings. Their home was uninhabitable. They had no insurance. They have only one part-time income. Yet they were determined to make the best of it, and to focus on the positive. They still had each other. They still had several acres of farmland on which they planned to build a more permanent home. They had been showered with gifts and kindness. Friends had offered them a house-sit for several months – and being in a town for a while would bring new opportunities. The fire had accelerated their building plans. The loss had given them a chance to start afresh, and to release the old energy from their past. It had swept them clean, and clarified their priorities. They trusted that everything was unfolding perfectly, even if they did not yet fully understand how. They were not denying their sense of grief and loss – but they had already turned Sunny Side Up. It was clear that the fire would yield many precious pearls.

Could they have prevented the fire? Almost certainly. Did they have warning signs of an impending crisis? In retrospect, yes. (Just as I had glanced at my fuel gauge as I set off for that workshop.) But using hindsight can easily lead to guilt, blame or recriminations – which keep you stuck in the world of judgment. The Universe makes no judgments. It never ascribes blame or guilt. Once an event has occurred, the Universe immediately charts a new course from where you are now. It knows what you want. It organises all the events and circumstances that you need. It ensures there are hidden gifts in every situation. All you need to do is get in the flow – and in time, that crisis might appear to have been carefully planned by the cosmos, since so many benefits have emerged from it. And perhaps a greater plan *was* unfolding.

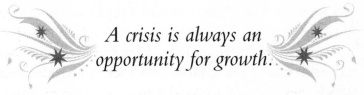

A crisis is always an opportunity for growth.

The future can never be preordained in a cosmos based upon free will and the law of attraction. You are always free to choose which future to create; but certain events become probable *unless* you change your vibrations. Once an event becomes inevitable, this grace-filled cosmos aligns itself to make the very best use of it. Powerful experiences lead to powerful desires, which create bold new futures. And every crisis is an opportunity for growth and transformation.

A friend who had a serious car accident fell in love with a nurse who cared for him in hospital, and sometimes jokes that he had to half-kill himself to meet his wife. The Universe could, of course, have found another way of getting them together – but at that time, he needed a break from work so that he could reassess and change direction, and had ignored the warning signs to take a holiday. He was also ready for a long-term partner, after many unsatisfying relationships which had helped him clarify his true desires. A car crash neatly dovetailed his needs, and matched his mixed vibrations at that time.

This loving cosmos can always make the best of things. Never waste a moment on regrets; it only increases your resistance. Just look forward to where you are going. And trust that everything really is working out for the best, whatever happens. After all, the Universe has the distinct advantage of seeing and knowing everything! If things *seem* to be going wrong, it is only because you cannot yet see the bigger picture. Just wait – and trust. As Serge Kahili King – a Hawaiian shaman I trained with long ago – is fond of saying: 'EWOP'. Everything Works Out Perfectly.

Everything works out
perfectly.

Does this mean that you don't need to follow your emotional guidance, since life will unfold beautifully whatever you do? It depends on whether you want your life to be a happy-ever-after fairytale, a disaster movie, or something in between. If you want to create heaven on earth, feeling your way into the flow is the easiest and smoothest way to go about it.

If you ignore your emotional guidance, you might find yourself on a rocky and troublesome path. As
continued …

you detour from the fast lane, and take a slip-road on to a bumpy and twisting country lane, you might lose your way for a while, or slow down to a crawl as you navigate around the deep ruts and floods. But there will be angels, guides and signposts all around, nudging you in the right direction from wherever you find yourself. Along the way, you will gain new skills, strengths and insights that will serve you in future. Your relationships might shift, or new people come into your life. You might recover your lost dreams and potential, or build even bigger dreams. You might get stuck in a rut for months or years (or even for several lifetimes) – but you are an eternal being. No big deal. There will be many pearls scattered along your chosen route. And your detour means that your future will sparkle even more brightly, as a result of your fresh clarity and desires.

In a loving Universe, nothing can ever go wrong.

Gathering pearls

In a loving Universe, there are no wrong paths, just smooth or rocky paths. On the smoother paths, you're in the flow and have a fabulous time. On the rockier paths, you learn and grow, and give birth to new desires and new futures. So even the bad times are good. Every problem is an opportunity. No experience is ever wasted. Everything that happens is a gift. You are intimately known and deeply loved by the cosmos. The Universe is incurably romantic, and wants you to live happily-ever-after. It believes in fairytales – with good reason, since it can make them come true. But even fairytale characters go through contrast on their way to sublime happiness, and so do we.

I sometimes imagine my higher self sitting on top of a hill, blowing dandelion clocks and humming a happy tune. Whatever happens in my life, she knows that it is working out fine, and she trusts in me to reach towards her, again and again. If I fall into deep contrast, it simply means my higher self has more expansive dreams for me now – she strolls across to an even bigger hill – and patiently waits for me to join her in those dreams. From her vantage point, everything looks good. She doesn't see any problems, imperfections or feet of clay. She only sees the beauty and emerging gifts. She knows I am gathering pearls. And she calls me softly towards her.

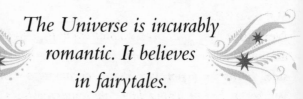

The Universe is incurably romantic. It believes in fairytales.

The more we have respect for times of chaos, pain and darkness in our lives, the sooner we gather the pearls. (As we shall see in the next chapter, this applies to global problems too.) This means not judging, not blaming, not resisting – forever trusting in our journey, appreciating what we can, loving ourselves and feeling our way back into the flow. Life is perfect in its imperfection; that is how it evolves. Life will never be exactly as you want it to be, or you would stop growing. There will always be unfulfilled desires you are reaching towards. There will always be bumpy times along the way. So enjoy the journey.

Wherever you are right now is just fine. Nothing can ever go wrong. You cannot mess it up. Whatever you choose, everything unfolds perfectly – not just for you, but for *everyone* involved. Your happiness can never interfere with anyone else's, since everyone has their own flow. The cosmos can deliver everyone's gifts. Isn't that wondrously elegant? Isn't it amazing how this loving and conscious Universe is designed? Doesn't it make you glow with warmth and gratitude?

Just for you

SUNNY SIDE UP
Next time you face any situation that is painful, frustrating, disappointing or challenging, remind yourself to see the light side. Focus on what you desire or appreciate, not on what you see as bad or wrong. Here are some questions that can flip you to the Sunny Side Up:

✧ *How does this help me clarify what I want?*

✧ *How can I make this a small deal instead of a Big Deal?*

✧ *How can I appreciate myself in this situation?*

✧ *What am I grateful for in this experience? What are the blessings?*

✧ *What is the opportunity here?*

Gathering the pearls

Look back at the most troubled periods of your life, or the greatest challenges you have faced — times when you might have faced a rollercoaster of emotions. Can you see the gifts that emerged? Perhaps inner strengths and resources, self-awareness, new skills and knowledge, greater depth and intimacy in relationships, or the ability to honour your own needs and emotions? What dreams and desires did that situation clarify or intensify for you? What 'chance' encounters or happy coincidences emerged during or after that period? What pearls have you gathered from your times of contrast? Trust that, whatever comes your way in future, there will be more pearls to gather and dreams to ripen — and the Universe will offer signposts all along the way. Know that, whatever happens, you are deeply loved.

Chapter Eight

You *Can* Make a Difference

*As our hearts open, our talents and gifts begin to blossom. **Marianne Williamson**[39]*

Once upon a time, there was a wise woman in the mountains who found a precious stone in a stream. The next day she met a traveller who was hungry, and opened her bag to share her food. The hungry traveller saw the precious stone, and asked if she might give it to him. She did so without hesitation. The traveller left rejoicing in his good fortune, since he knew the stone could bring him financial security for life. But a few days later, he came back in search of the woman. 'I know how valuable this stone is', he said, 'but I'm returning it to you, in the hope that you can give me something even more precious. I want whatever it is in you that allowed you to give me this stone.'

What was this precious gift in her? *It was her connection to Source energy.* This gave her an ability to love freely. It gave her a sense of empowerment. It gave her faith in abundance. Like the Universe, the wise woman gave whatever was asked – but without making any sacrifice. She knew there was a limitless supply. And she had already bestowed a priceless gift to the traveller; she had woken him up.

Our greatest gift to others is our state of consciousness. It is more precious than glimmering gold or glittering jewels. It has the power to transform. As you feel your way into the flow, you stop trying to prove yourself worthy, or living a life carved out for you by others. You shift more and more into love-mode. You discover what makes your heart sing. Your energy becomes coherent. You become joyful and passionate. You breathe more easily. You feel inspired and creative and free. Then there is a feeling of rightness, a sense that you are on your true path, that you are doing whatever you came here to do. You are living in harmony with your soul.

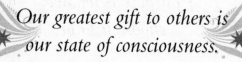

Our greatest gift to others is our state of consciousness.

Your higher purpose

Countless people have said to me with a sigh, 'I wish I knew my higher purpose.' You will have entered this lifetime with certain intentions – and when you live in harmony with those intentions, you will feel great and doors will open easily. But the *form* that your purpose takes is entirely up to you, and even its essence is highly flexible. Your purpose is whatever you choose it to be. It is not a mysterious secret to be discovered. It is not a task or mission handed down to you from on high. It is whatever naturally emerges from your unique combination of strengths, talents and experiences – and if you follow your bliss, you will find it.

How might your love for animals mesh with your computer know-how, languages and experience of world travel? Or how might your background of childhood abuse fit with your training as a nurse, and your love of singing or ceramics? When you rise each morning buzzing with anticipation, and you are doing what you would do if you didn't need an income, you know that you have found your life's work. And it will keep unfolding as you change and grow.

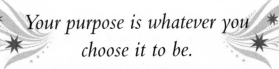

Your purpose is whatever you choose it to be.

I still feel amazed and privileged that I am paid to write books, give talks, see clients and run *Living Magically* workshops – all of which I adore. I decided 15 years ago only to say yes to invitations that feel exciting, and never to do anything for the money. I organise my life *as if* I didn't have to earn a living, and I do whatever I love. I read inspiring books that I would read anyway, explore fascinating ideas, attend uplifting workshops and conferences, visit wondrous places and have deep and riveting conversations – and I get to call it work! It all feels like play to me. I also know that my own personal growth and experiences are central to my work, so even when life is challenging, I trust that the gifts will be greater than I can imagine, and will indirectly help many others. Sometimes I think I am a painfully slow learner, as I gradually integrate what I teach into my own life – but we teach what we need to learn! I've been thanked by thousands of people for changing their lives or inspiring them, but it still thrills me each time I open a grateful card or email. It is deeply rewarding to know that my work touches and transforms so many lives.

Each of us is a unique piece in this giant cosmic jigsaw – and every part is needed to make the whole. If you are reading this, your higher purpose is probably linked to the current evolution in human consciousness. You are quite likely to be a teacher-healer, whatever form that takes – that is, someone who inspires others into releasing their resistance and expanding their awareness. Perhaps you are involved in health, psychology, education, science, religion or spirituality, international relations, business, the law, politics, ecology, the media or the creative or performing arts – and your purpose is to bring love, higher awareness, new perspectives or standards of excellence into that field. Perhaps your work is apparently mundane, such as making furniture – yet the joy and creativity that you pour into it makes *your* cupboards and chairs sparkle with an uplifting energy. Perhaps you are a sales assistant or receptionist or accountant, but you are fully present to everyone that you meet – or radiate enthusiasm, inner peace or love – so that you subtly shift their consciousness.

You can fulfil your higher purpose through any kind of work. Whenever you hold a higher state of awareness, you send out a high-frequency note like a tuning fork, to which others can then resonate. You become a catalyst for change. Then the impact you have upon others – *whatever* you choose to do – will be inspiring, helpful and constructive. Like the wise woman with the stone, *what you do* is far less important than *who you are*: your state of being.

As your vibrations climb the emotional ladder (see chapter 3), your heart opens, you feel more enthusiastic and passionate, your vision expands, you feel more and more empowered – and your actions are guided more and more by intuition and joy. Then you step into your higher purpose. You reach towards your higher self. And by choosing to do what you love, rather than working to pay the bills, or doing what others want or expect, you make a difference – simply by making that heart-centred choice. By honouring yourself. By being guided from within. The word enthusiasm comes from the Greek *en theos*, meaning the god within. As you do what you love, you align with Source energy – and your creativity bursts forth.

 *As you do what you love, you align with Source energy.*

Many people want to know their higher purpose because they want to be of service to the world. It is wonderful to be involved in creative projects, to give a helping hand, to inspire others, to use our gifts and talents, to offer constructive ideas and fresh visions, and even to challenge dysfunctional systems and beliefs. It is natural for us to want to make a difference, and to have a sense of belonging and participation. However, I am wary of the concept of 'world service'– despite its popularity in New Age philosophy. It can be fuelled by the fearful ego's need to feel good, worthy and righteous, or to justify your own existence. Some people even believe that you should not get paid for such work – which suggests that some work is so special and elevated that you should not expect something as 'merely mortal' as money in return for your time, energy and talents. (Spot the arrogance and superiority in that!) It can also raise anxiety that you might get black marks in the afterlife if you don't 'fulfil your mission' – which means you can forget that *the purpose of life is joy*. If you follow your bliss, it ensures that your healthy ego is aligned with your higher self. Then you will make a positive difference.

Beyond right and wrong

Before you jump on any world-changing bandwagon, it is worth questioning your motives. For example, much of the well-meaning but destructive action in the world comes from righteous anger. Self-righteousness is a fairly high vibration for the fear-based ego, so it likes to hang out there! Anger can fire you up when your vibrations are very low – perhaps in shame, insecurity, grief, anxiety, guilt or despair. Anger, righteousness and blame come as a welcome relief when you feel disempowered, or have identified with others who feel helpless. There is a positive role for anger. It can draw attention to what needs to change. It can be a stepping stone towards self-respect and empowerment, and get things moving – but it is not a place to remain for long.

One problem with righteousness is that you expect others to see it *your* way – which means you cannot listen with an open heart. You just want others to agree with you. When I was a crusading vegetarian, I believed that no one should eat meat – and I could trot out all the health, ecological, economic and ethical reasons why! I still choose to be vegetarian, 30 years on, but I'm much more reluctant to poke my nose into other people's business, or to try to control the world. My choices are my own, and what anyone else does is none of my business. No one can know what is right for anyone else, or what their Path is – and I am glad that we live on a planet where most of us are free to choose, and there is such an interesting variety of lifestyles, values and points of view. I no longer need others to agree with me. In fact,

I *like* people being different from me. How dull the world would be if everyone had the same opinions and beliefs!

Our higher self celebrates and enjoys diversity, but the fearful ego treats difference as a problem or threat. If someone has a different perspective, and we are locked into fear-mode, we tend to ask who is right and who is wrong, or who is good and who is bad, or who is better and who is worse. And we want to be the one who is good and right and better. The one who is beyond reproach. It doesn't matter whether it is a discussion about how to raise children, or recycling rubbish, or what kind of job you do, the fear-based ego tends to feel either one-up or one-down – either putting others down in order to feel good and worthy, or feeling inadequate by comparison. When you need to see yourself as good and perfect, someone else must be bad, wrong or inadequate – rather than simply *different*. Different needs, values, priorities, beliefs and opinions. The truth is that everyone is good and right from their own point of view, if only you listen with an open and compassionate heart. If only you think like the Universe.

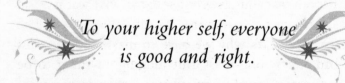

*To your higher self, everyone
is good and right.*

Pushing against or reaching towards

When your vibrations hover around self-righteousness, you are in fear-mode, so you tend to *push against* the negative, instead of *reaching towards* what is positive. You criticise, complain and find fault. You motivate others to change through fear, duty or guilt, rather than through love, joy and inspiration. You try to control or exclude what you see as bad or threatening. Just like those you criticise, you are insisting, 'I am right and you are wrong.' You might even justify harming others on the grounds that you *know* you are in the right! This is conditional love. You want someone else or the world to change so that you can feel happy and content – instead of becoming happy and content so that reality can change. You are trying to change the world from the outside-in. Then you attract more of the same. As you rant and rail against anything, you attune to its vibrations. Then you become part of the problem, instead of part of the solution.

Personally I don't like macaroni cheese; but I don't want everyone else to agree with me, or insist that it is banned from restaurants. I simply don't eat it. We can be discerning about our own choices, without being judgmental about others' choices or priorities. 'Oh, but macaroni cheese is a trivial example', you might argue. 'What about war? Surely *everyone* agrees that war is a bad thing?' Well, apparently not – or all nations would be at peace. 'But that's why we have to make people *realise* how bad and wrong it is!' But judging anything to be bad and wrong simply gets us more stuck in the mire. It is not thinking like the Universe – which makes no judgments, which is always understanding and compassionate. War must be serving some people's needs, or it would cease immediately; and, in a Universe based on the law of attraction, there are no victims. Certainly, no one could drop bombs while fully connected to Source – but those involved in war do invariably see themselves as 'in the right'. And our righteous indignation about their 'bad' behaviour will not help the situation! It comes from the same level of consciousness. It comes from duality, from judgment. Pushing against war can never lead us towards peace.

> *When you push against anything, you increase its power.*

I recently co-founded a project to bring universal spirituality to a local Anglican church. A group of us offers weekly meetings that are creation-centred, joyful, inspiring and celebratory: a spirituality of unconditional love that crosses the boundaries between faiths. (Which is perhaps closer to what Jesus really taught, or might teach today, than what we call Christianity.) We might offer a Celtic blessing, a Sufi poem, a native American chant, a Jewish or Aramaic prayer, a circle dance, a healing ritual or visualisation, a Taizé chant, inspired thoughts and reflections, shared silence and lighting of candles. The usual Sunday morning services run alongside these new meetings, for those who are comfortable with the old theology. Instead of labelling the Church as bad or wrong, we recognise that it is meeting some people's needs and has its own strengths. (Trying to be good *does* make you feel better when your vibrations hover around shame, guilt or insecurity.) Like any religion, it is the right path for many people. Our aim is to be integrative, and honour everyone's needs. We are aware of how religious dogma based on fear, guilt, control and judgment limits and distorts us, but we do not push against it – which would merely increase resistance to change. We accept what is, while reaching towards a loving and empowering vision of what might be.

This marks a sweeping change in my own consciousness. For many years, I battled *against* the old paradigm in health, psychology, religion and education. I explored what was *wrong* with the old approaches – allopathic medicine and psychiatry, mainstream psychology, patriarchal religion and left-brained education – and criticised them at great length. Like any crusader, I felt sure I was in the right! Then I slowly came to understand that they symbolised parts of me that were stuck and reaching out for love. Parts of me that were lost in fear and judgment. And like any Shadow selves, perhaps they had wisdom and other gifts for me. But the more I criticised, the more these parts curled up, or fired hostility back at me.

Slowly I came to know teachers, doctors and ministers whom I loved and cared about as friends, and to respect and appreciate their work – and realised that our models are not so far apart after all. Even when they are, everyone has something positive to offer. My old defences and boundaries began to melt. I still want to see the world change, but I no longer want to control or criticise others. I do slip into old habits at times; but when I catch myself seeing problems or fault, I now aim to reach out with love and understanding. I aim to build bridges. Or sometimes I just tell myself to back off, mind my own business, and accept others as they are!

There is a limited role for analysing what is 'wrong', for exploring the underlying causes of a problem – but we have to see through the eyes of Love. We need to shift our own consciousness first. As Gandhi said, we have to become the change we want to see in the world. Finding fault with others (or even worse, with ourselves) destroys our inner peace – and it is inner peace that will make global peace possible. The only way to promote change is through unconditional love. Love that is accepting and embracing, rather than excluding or rejecting. Love that heals wounds and divisions. Love that listens with an open heart. Love that is respectful and inclusive. Love that honours what is, while holding a vision for the future.

Until you reach out with love and compassion towards those who might seem stuck, or even to be acting in negative or destructive ways, or who simply have a different viewpoint, you are playing the same old games of us-and-them. Battle games. Enemy thinking. You are living from the old cosmology, which promotes fear and separation rather than love and connectedness. When you are connected to Source, you feel secure, worthy and loving – and are loving and respectful of others. You can then become an incredible force for social change. Instead of being a protester, you become a dreamer and visionary.

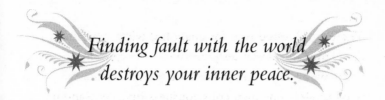

Finding fault with the world destroys your inner peace.

Taking responsibility

Whatever your concerns about the world, it is worth asking whether these mirror your own issues. If you worry about world peace, do you need to focus on finding inner peace? If you fret about child abuse, do you abuse your own inner child – perhaps by ignoring your feelings, or working too hard? If your concern is the world's starving, how do you starve or deprive yourself? If you champion the powerless and vulnerable, how do you give away your own power? If you worry about pollution, do you pollute your own consciousness with negative thoughts? What do you need to clean up? Is the problem really outside you – or is it within?

This is not an *alternative* to taking global action, but it is something to think about. Once your own issues are resolved – or you are simply more aware of them – you will be less *troubled* by world issues. You are less likely to be stuck in painful duality, and can take global action from a higher level of consciousness.

Is the problem really outside you – or is it within?

HELPING OR RESCUING?

People who want to help others or change the world often grew up feeling responsible for others' happiness and well-being. This might sound compassionate and helpful, but it carries hidden dangers. It often means seeking a sense of self-worth through caring for others – and there is a thin line between helping and rescuing. We are 'rescuing' whenever we try to do things *for* people, instead of helping them to help themselves, or when we sacrifice our own needs for others, or try to protect them, or believe that we know what is best for anyone else. Instead of teaching someone how to fish, we might bring a fish round to their door every day (and congratulate ourselves for being so generous and charitable). Instead of asking why someone is having headaches, we might hand them a paracetamol – covering up the cause with an external solution. Instead of expecting someone to deal with their fear or insecurity, we might shelter them from the 'big bad wolves' – or try to change external conditions *for them* – which not only maintains the cause, but reinforces the idea that the other is weak, power-less or under threat. We collude in seeing the problem as outside them.[40]

Everyone has the power to make their own dreams come true. You cannot control anyone else's vibrations, so you cannot be responsible for their happiness or well-being. If you try to change anyone else's life from the outside, you are pushing against the river.

Often it feels wonderful to give someone gifts, or reach out and help, or to offer love and compassion, in which case they have attracted you as a vehicle for making that happen. You are responding to their vibrations, and everyone will be happy. But if it feels heavy, frustrating, constricting, inhibiting, driven, compulsive, tiring or virtuous – or if they seem to resist your 'help', or simply feel entitled to it – then you are being over-responsible. You are rescuing instead of helping.

Rescuing means you might be trying to make *yourself* feel better, or seeking approval or admiration. It means you might be taking sides in a drama, instead of seeing the whole picture – perhaps seeing someone as helpless or as a victim. You might be imposing your own moral agenda on others, instead of minding your own business. You might be seeing yourself as stronger, wiser or more resourceful – which disempowers them, since the truth is that everyone has their own connection to Source, and needs to follow their own guidance and become self-empowered. Rescuing means you are keeping them stuck, rather than helping them to grow and change.

Since you cannot control others' vibrations, you cannot control what they create.

As I write this chapter, the head of the Catholic Church in England is calling for people to eat less in solidarity with the world's poor. I am left scratching my head in amazement! His suggestion fits with the old theology of guilt, sacrifice and redemption – but how can anyone imagine that *more* people going hungry or depriving themselves somehow makes the world a better place? Would it make sense to make ourselves ill in solidarity with those who are sick? Or to say goodbye to our loved ones in solidarity with those who are lonely? Should we give up our happiness and optimism in sympathy with those who are miserable and negative? Would that really help anyone? It is crazy thinking. It simply means that more people disconnect from the limitless abundance and love of the Universe – then try to reconnect and redeem themselves by being good. It drags us down. It lowers the world's vibrations. It also comes from the limiting belief that the world is a solid reality with only so much to go around – so if you have more, others have less – which is a great recipe for guilt. Why not just feel *grateful* for the gifts and abundance in our lives? Then we add to the gratitude and joy of humanity.

The mystic Meister Eckhart said, 'If the only prayer you said in your life was thank you, that would suffice.' Gratitude and appreciation are very high vibrations, which align you with your higher self; they open you to receive gifts. Self-sacrifice will always split your energy; it pushes your gifts away. If you support beliefs in lack and scarcity, and the practice of self-denial and martyrhood, that is what you help to create in the world. If you hold the vibrations of prosperity and health and loving rela-tionships, that is what you help to create in the world.

If I allow more to flow into my own life, I help others open to receiving.

NURTURING YOURSELF

You cannot give to others from an empty cup. If you try to take action while pushing through resistance, it always backfires. You begin to feel resentful, trapped and exhausted. Like a hamster on a treadwheel, you try harder and harder, but make little progress. You develop a sense of urgency, or even desperation. It becomes addictive, and difficult to stop. (I know – I've been there!) You might feel virtuous, but you will rarely reach the higher echelons of the emotional ladder. If you see your work as an assigned task or mission, or it becomes a false source of worthiness and redemption, it is easy to think you have never done enough or given enough – which is a slippery slope towards workaholism and burnout. You are seeing life as a mission, instead of a gift.

Some years ago, I remember an inner voice telling me sternly, 'You are not here to live your life. You are here to serve the world!' In shock, I recognised this nose-to-the-grindstone voice as coming from life-is-a-trial mythology – a well-meaning but judgmental part of me that had been in charge for a long time.[41] I knew it was only trying to help – but instead of bowing down to its harsh demands and continuing to work long hours, I resolved to shift my energy.

I still passionately want to change the world – to see a world of unconditional love, joy, freedom and spiritual awareness – but I now know that promoting love begins with self-love. And promoting freedom in the world begins with setting myself free. Enough is enough – and I would now rather write a handful of inspiring books while enjoying life to the full than write countless mediocre books borne of self-sacrifice. What is more, I will be far more effective as a writer, more fun to be around, and live longer! We cannot inspire anyone unless we are connected to Source. *Everything* depends upon our vibrations. The higher you climb up the emotional ladder, the more you can give.

The good news is that – if you want to make a difference in the world – you have to be committed to following your bliss, nurturing yourself and keeping your life in balance. Every day should feel like a vacation, whether or not it is a 'working' day. These days, I only say yes to what feels good. If someone makes a request and I feel resistance, then I know it is not in the flow. Their vibrations are not aligned with what I can offer, or they are stuck in victimhood, fear or anger, and I would be rescuing rather than helping. Or perhaps the timing is not right. Helping someone or saying yes always feels joyful when it is in the flow – then you both benefit from the action. If it doesn't feel good, the rule is that it isn't serving either of you. You are flowing against the river. As always, *nothing is more important than how you feel.* Your primary responsibility is towards yourself – towards staying connected to Source.

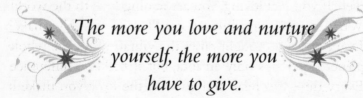

The more you love and nurture yourself, the more you have to give.

Right now, I could probably finish writing this chapter – but instead I'm off to meet a friend in a teashop. After a cappuccino and cheesecake, and an hour or two of nour-ishing conversation, perhaps I will find more inspiring words than if I had remained dutifully at my computer. Perhaps not. But I no longer feel I have to justify taking time out for a walk, a massage, Qi Gong class or social-ising. I do not have to justify my existence through work or childcare – through giving to others. My life belongs to me at last. Dealing with my in-tray is less important than walking in the mountains, or flying a kite with my child. Writing can wait until tomorrow. Or the next day. Or whenever it feels delightful to write. And on some days, I write into the small hours – so happily absorbed in ideas and creativity that time dissolves.

Envision a golden future

While you feel happy, loving and appreciative, you *are* making a positive difference – even while wandering alone in the countryside, sitting in a teashop or petting your cat – since your energy is inseparable from the rest of the Universe. You belong to the interconnected web of life. If you feel joyful, you contribute joy to the energetic web. If you feel loving, you are adding love to the world. What better contribution could you possibly make? Every positive thought raises the vibrations of the whole planet – perhaps only an iota, but it makes a difference. Every time you relax and go with the flow, you make it slightly easier for others to do so. And every time you reach out with love and gratitude, the angels sing – since you are helping to create heaven on earth.

Conversely every time you judge yourself, others or the world, you add to the negativity in the world. Every time you feel fearful about ecological problems or global conflicts or the future of humanity – or even your personal safety and security – you increase the fear and anxiety in the world. Every time you watch the TV news, and tell yourself that the world is becoming more uncaring, violent, sick or downright awful, you deepen the pool of negative thoughts. Every time you believe in lack, scarcity or competition – or sacrifice yourself for others – you are forgetting this is a limitless Universe. Whenever you worry about someone else, and mistakenly call this love, you are associating love with fear. You are cutting yourself off from unconditional love. You are promoting patterns that keep us locked in the world of fear. And you know that you're doing that because you *feel bad*. 'Oh, but I just feel bad because I feel so sorry for those people, or so worried about the state of the world, or because I care so much,' you might say. No, you don't. You feel bad because you are disconnecting from your higher self. And if you beat yourself up for doing that, you make it even worse! We are all human. We all slip into these habitual patterns of thought – so wake up, laugh softly, and remind yourself that everything is unfolding perfectly.

✳ *Become a dreamer and visionary for the planet.* ✳

As Eleanor Roosevelt said, 'The future belongs to those who believe in the beauty of their dreams.' It can be a delicate balancing act to become aware of global problems, and want to help make the world a better place, without dwelling on the negative. As in making your personal dreams come true, the trick is to turn your attention to what you wish to create, or how you envision the world to be, instead of focussing on what you see as bad or faulty.

Nothing is wrong. Nothing needs fixing. Everything is just in a state of unfolding, of evolution, of growth and change. Which is how it will always be – so you had better get used to it. When you see through the eyes of Love, you do not see any darkness. You only see the potential for more light. Then you focus like a laser beam on that future potential – and thus help to bring it into reality. Your higher self never focusses on problems, only on solutions.

At a global level, don't you imagine that whatever created this Universe and set the earth miraculously spinning in its orbit can also regulate the temperature of the planet, and help us find ways of dealing with radioactive waste, nuclear warheads and disappearing topsoil? The creative forces of the cosmos are limitless. Energy is infinitely flexible and mutable – but it is inextricably tied to consciousness. This is a psycho-energetic reality. If you worry about global warming and other ecological issues – or war, poverty, cancer or terrorism – you simply create more evidence of them. Worry is like a prayer, which attracts more of the same.

As we ask and relax, we are always guided towards solutions. We are sparks of God in action. In fact, perhaps we have created such global problems in order to *force* ourselves to expand into higher awareness – to see the bigger picture, to discover the creative power of thought, to go beyond our old limitations, to reconnect with love and faith and trust – since problems cannot be resolved at the level of consciousness at which they are created.

We are apprentice gods and goddesses – who give birth to desires and visions that we *can* then manifest, whether personally or globally. If you can imagine and believe it, it can happen. Nothing comes into being unless it is first conjured up in someone's imagination, so devote time to daydreaming. The world does not need worriers, fearmongers or critics – but it does need dreamers. So become a loving visionary for the planet. And begin by taking responsibility for creating your own slice of heaven on earth – by making your own life as heavenly as you can imagine it to be.

Just for you

FINDING YOUR HIGHER PURPOSE

What makes your heart sing? What do you love to do? What brings you most joy? What are your strengths and talents? What fires up your passion and enthusiasm? How do you wish to see the world evolve? Make sure you are not trying to be good, worthy or righteous; or finding fault with anyone; nor identifying with others and trying to rescue or protect them, instead of loving and nurturing yourself.

As you follow your bliss and focus upon your personal and global dreams, you move step-by-step towards your higher purpose – often by finding your own unique combination of talents, knowledge and experience. We teach what we most need to learn – so don't tell yourself that your life must be sorted out before you can embark on your higher purpose. Our greatest 'imperfections' are often the source of our greatest gifts. Life is never perfect! It is always unfolding. Whatever you long to do, begin it now.

BIRTHING ENERGY INTO FORM
Make yourself comfortable, and relax deeply. Choose a dream that you want to become a reality. It might be a global dream such as peace between troubled nations, or saving the rainforests, or kindness towards animals. Or it might be a personal dream such as finding your dream job, becoming self-employed, writing a book or creating a work of art. Imagine this desire as if it were just energy – which it is – and visualise that energy. It might look like streaks of light, a kaleidoscope of colour, a brilliant star, separate blobs that stab at each other, or a splodge of muddy and formless energy. Now think about your dream, and how much you want it – and make the energy more beautiful, more colourful, more integrated or carefully formed, brighter or more spectacular. Use your imagination to turn that energy into a form that feels good and looks radiant.

Spend a few minutes each day on this – or as often as feels right – until the energy feels stable, brilliant and ready to birth, and whenever you think about your desire, you tingle with joyful anticipation. Then follow any intuitive impulses to take action. You are helping to birth a new future.

Chapter Nine

Dare to Live, Dare to Dream

*The challenge is to dare to believe your dreams
in the centre of illusion.* **Emmanuel**[42]

If you want to create your own heaven on earth, begin right now. Love what is, while reaching towards what might be. Live every day to the full – drinking it like a glass of champagne, and appreciating every sip. Do not postpone happiness, love or freedom until some future date – when life has moved on, or a problem is resolved, or you have more free time, or have found your soul mate, or the children are older, or that project is finished, or your in-tray is empty. The right time never comes. The in-tray is never empty. Life slips by while you are waiting – and you get into the habit of waiting for life to be different, waiting for something to change, or waiting for someone else's permission to be free. Then you hold the vibrations of your higher self and its dreams at bay. Just around the corner.

'Tell me, what is it you plan to do with your one wild and precious life?', asks poet Mary Oliver.[43] Your life is happening right now. This is it! This is *your* adventure in consciousness. It is a divine gift to you. So what do you wish to do with it today? And tomorrow? And this year? What fills you with joy and delight? What do you love to do? Who do you adore spending time with? Where do you love to be? What delicious experiences would you like to have? What is your holy longing? What are your wildest dreams? Whatever you long to do, begin it now. Or keep imagining and expecting what you desire until you tingle with anticipation, and pull it into your reality.

Where in the world would you like to go? The Greek islands? The Taj Mahal? San Francisco? The Grand Canyon? The Great Wall of China? Easter Island? The Seychelles? The temples of Bangkok? Machu Picchu? What do you dream of doing? Diving in a coral reef? Trekking in the Himalayas? Crossing the Sahara by camel? Going on African safari? River-rafting in Colorado? Seeing reindeer in Lapland? Swimming in the Dead Sea? Souk shopping in Marrakech? Or perhaps you long to play the saxophone, or sculpt wood, or go firewalking? Or build your own home? Or live on a South Seas island? Or set up an organic farm? This planet is rich with wondrous possibilities. Why not start planning your next adventure, juicy experience or creative outlet today?[44] (Or are you already coming up with reasons why not? *Can't afford it. Can't spare the time. Too many commitments. Not fit enough. Too scared. Maybe next year. That sounds lovely, but…*) If you avoid change and stick to your usual routines, you will stick to your usual thoughts. Your desires fade, and you fall asleep. Travel, variety and freshness can shake up your old habits, and wake you up.

You can do, be or have anything that you desire. Life will never be perfect, since it is always in a state of unfolding. It is always moving on, changing, expanding – as you move from desires to reality to new desires. You will always be reaching for more. That is how the Universe evolves. Nothing is wrong, and we are all doing fine. You will never reach your destination, so you have to enjoy the journey. Enjoy every step. Fall madly in love with life. Live for today, and reach towards an even more wonderful tomorrow.

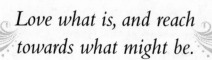

Love what is, and reach towards what might be.

Whatever is happening right now, you can feel good about it – by finding more positive thoughts, and going with the flow. When you change your life from the inside out – by transforming your inner world – you find true freedom and unconditional love. Once you are happy without condition, you are truly free. Then you set others free too, and become a source of joy and inspiration to those around you. You are helping to co-create heaven on earth.

This world is not a solid and mundane place. It is a magical reality that responds energetically to your thoughts, your desires, your imagination. You are a dream-weaver, moulding your future with every thought – so choose your thoughts wisely. Whatever you believe, you will prove yourself right. Listen to the voices of fear and doubt, and you will remain imprisoned by being good, conforming or staying safe. Listen to the voice of Love, and you will believe in happy-ever-after fairytales. Listen to the voice of Love, and you can make every dream come true. You can become a butterfly.

You are deeply loved and cherished by the Universe – and it is always on your side. Love is life believing in itself. So believe in yourself, and set yourself free. Accept that life is a gift, and feel your way into the flow. Make a habit of feeling good. Dare to break the rules. Dare to live your own life. Dare to be different. Dare to follow your bliss. Dare to live creatively. Dare to love passionately. Dare to reach out and connect. Dare to trust. Dare to dance and to dream. Dare to be a visionary. And watch the miracles unfold.

Dare to live. Dare to love.
Dare to dream.

Twelve guidelines for creating your own heaven on earth

Follow these guidelines for just 21 days – and watch your life transform:

1. **Accept life as a gift.** You do not have to earn or deserve love (or joy, or success, or money, or anything else). You are not here to please anyone else. The Universe wants you – yes, you personally! – to be deliriously happy. Whatever you ask for, the Universe immediately says yes. All you have to do is to get out of your own way.

2. **Clarify your desires.** There are no impossible dreams. If you have any heartfelt desire – and can believe and expect it – you can dream it into being. What are your dreams? What do you want, and why do you want it? (If you have lost touch with your dreams, follow some of the other guidelines here until your vibrations are higher, so that your vision expands.)

3. **Feel your way into the flow.** Nothing matters more than feeling good, since that is your personal indicator of your connection

continued ...

to Source. Trust your emotional guidance. Choose thoughts and actions that feel joyful, soothing, self-loving and liberating. Be true to yourself. Don't try to be good or perfect. Don't be swayed into pleasing others at the expense of your own needs and desires. Don't try to control, restrict or manipulate others so that you feel better; it always backfires. Remember that anger can be a positive stepping stone when you feel disempowered – but it is just a stepping stone. Listen to the inner voice of Love. Climb your emotional ladder. Change your world from the inside out, not from the outside in.

4. **Become a laser beam.** You get what you focus upon, so think about what you desire – rather than what is bad, wrong or lacking, why it is unlikely to happen, what your block- ages and issues are, how others are preventing it, why you feel sorry for yourself, what you regret or how your past has messed you up, or finding fault with yourself, others or the world. Catch any negative thoughts, and turn them around. Make a list of memories, thoughts, snippets of conversations, ideas and stories that support what you desire – which help you think positively and expect it to happen.

continued …

Read your list daily – or ponder it happily
in your imagination – and keep reminding
yourself. Refuse to entertain any fear, doubt or
uncertainty about your desire. Believe in your
dreams. (Tip: When you focus purely on your
desire, it always feels good.)

5. **Follow your bliss**. Fill your days with
   activities, people, places and projects that
   you love, that make you feel good, which
   bring out all that is best in you. Live your life
   – more and more – as if you were on
   vacation. Never postpone living your dreams,
   or you might wait forever. Do it now! Give
   up struggle, efforting and duty – or feeling
   responsible for anyone else's happiness. Relax
   more. Laugh more. Play more. Have more
   fun. Nourish yourself with joy. Follow your
   energy, doing whatever feels good in this
   moment. Adore yourself!

6. **Appreciate everything and everyone**.
   Count your blessings. Be thankful for all that
   is wonderful in your life, and for the joy and
   beauty in each moment. Take time to smell the
   roses. Express your gratitude and appreciation
   of others. Assume that everyone is good and
   loving. Focus on what is best in people. And
   continued …

take care to appreciate yourself. Recognise how well you are doing. Acknowledge your strengths. Never beat yourself up. Treat yourself with the unconditional love, compassion and respect that the Universe has for you.

7. **Accept what is**. Love your life as it is, even though it isn't perfect right now (since it never will be!). Focus on what is good in your life. Even if you are in crisis, or having a hard time, take a deep breath and relax into it. If you can, laugh about it. Don't battle against it – or against any negative emotion. Make peace with what is. In a loving cosmos, no experience is ever wasted. Blessings will come from this time. You are gathering precious pearls. Whatever we resist persists – so the more deeply you accept it, the more quickly it can pass. *And it will pass.*

8. **Devote time to happy daydreams**. Get yourself into a happy mood, then visualise what you want for 15 minutes or so each day. During the day, keep imagining that you already have that ideal job or home, your lover is in the next room, you are vibrantly healthy or your bank account is full to bursting. Feel the joy. More and more, begin to resonate with

continued ...

that future self, rather than with your current reality.

9. **Meditate daily.** Or use an active form of meditation such as tai chi, dancing, jogging or yoga – anything that calms or empties your mind, or helps you focus on your breath or movement. (And don't beat yourself up when you forget or cannot find the time! No big deal.)

10. **Surround yourself with support**. Avoid anyone who throws you into fear, guilt, anger or self-doubt, or who drains your energy – just for now. Until you know you can raise your own vibrations regardless. Until you move beyond defensiveness. (Or at least stop blaming them for keeping you out of the flow! Only you can do that.) Open yourself to new relationships. Reach out to others. Spend time with those who make you feel cherished and adored, who awaken and inspire you, who encourage you to follow your dreams. Cherish them in return. Support your body with nourishing and delicious food. Make your home a beautiful and relaxing place to be – a sanctuary of peace and love. Clear out any clutter. Read inspirational books. Use affirmation cards.

continued …

Light a daily candle to remind you of your dreams.

11. **Act from vision, joy and inspiration.**
Once you feel happy, follow any intuitive urges to take action. If you are feeling less than hopeful, shift your energy before taking action or making a decision. Make sure you are in love-mode. If you want to make a difference in the world, focus on raising your own vibrations – on feeling good – rather than trying to change or control others. Then do whatever makes your heart sing.

12. **Act as if it is going to happen**. Make plans for the future as if it is a foregone conclusion that your dreams will come true. They might not happen in exactly the form that you expect, or when you expect – the Universe might have even better plans – but you can guarantee that if you ask, it is given.

Once you are in the flow, you will find yourself in the right place at the right time, saying or doing the right thing – and the Universe will shower you with its gifts.

Afterword

As soon as I finished writing this book, I travelled alone to Egypt and Jordan – visiting the pyramids and sphinx, wandering in the 'lost city' of Petra, snorkelling in the Red Sea and quad-biking into desert canyons. Day after day, I found myself in a state of profound joy, inner peace and gratitude – totally in love with life. It felt like heaven on earth.

On the day before going home, I journeyed to St Catherine's monastery in the Sinai desert, scene of the Biblical burning bush, where Moses is said to have received the Ten Commandments. I have long felt uneasy with the Ten Commandments, because of the negativity and judgment they carry, and their parental and imprisoning tone. Saying 'Thou shalt *not*...' is such bad psychology – guaranteed to throw people into shame, conflict or rebellion. (Try telling yourself 'Thou shalt *not* think of a white elephant' without picturing one.) Surely we could find more liberating, empowering and inspiring guidelines for our lives?

After lingering in the Eastern Orthodox chapel, I sat on a golden sandstone rock just outside the monastery walls, with Mount Sinai towering above me – and began to meditate. Almost immediately, I was filled to overflowing with joy and bliss (Source energy). Intuitively I reached for a notebook and pen. Then I heard an inner voice speak: 'Two thousand years ago, Jesus came to earth with a message of unconditional love – but few were ready to hear it. Humanity is now ready to receive that message. The time for commandments set in stone is past. The time for invitations has come. As one of many wayshowers for this new era, you will now be offered Ten Invitations to humanity as an alternative to the Ten Commandments – invitations based upon a spirituality of unconditional love, which restores the divine feminine. This period marks the dawning of a new heaven and a new earth.'[45]

For several hours afterwards, I found it almost impossible to speak. I was in such rapture that I felt like an angelic being, and half-wondered whether I must be glowing with light. People turned to smile at me, and children chased after me. As I returned home to the Lake District, that extraordinary joy remained with me, along with a thrilling sense of anticipation for what lies ahead – for me, for you and for our world.

Here are the Ten Invitations I received:

Ten Invitations

1   You are invited to love yourself, others and life without condition – trusting that, in an evolving Universe, everything is unfolding perfectly.

2   You are invited to do whatever makes your heart sing and your spirit dance. Only that.

3   You are invited to live fearlessly and passionately – to step into your divinity, while embracing your humanity.

4   You are invited to treat yourself and others with extraordinary respect and kindness – reaching out with love towards all beings, and seeing the Light within everyone.

5   You are invited to honour everyone else's beliefs, feelings, values and choices – valuing their uniqueness, and remembering that you cannot know their path or guidance.

6   You are invited to honour the earth, your body and all creation as sacred and divine – and to celebrate life in all its richness.

continued ...

7. You are invited to choose your own mission or purpose, expressing your creative gifts, talents and vision in whatever way feels most joyful.

8. You are invited to listen to the inner voice of Love, which always sets you free – knowing that your goodness and worthiness are never in question, and that you can do no wrong.

9. You are invited to trust in a loving and abundant Universe. *Ask and it is given. Seek and ye shall find. Knock and the door shall be opened.*

10. You are invited to follow your dreams and desires – trusting your feelings and using your imagination to create your own heaven on earth.

Endnotes

FOREWORD

1. Maggie Oman (ed.), *Prayers of Healing* (Conari Press, 1997), p.95. Manitongquat is a medicine man and storyteller from the Wampanoag tribe of New England.

2. Eg. See Paul H. Ray and Sherry Ruth Anderson, *The Cultural Creatives* (Three Rivers Press, 2000) or any of the constant stream of books about the emergent new paradigm over the past three decades.

CHAPTER ONE: LIFE IS A GIFT

3. From the teachings of Abraham. See www.abraham-hicks. com, or Esther and Jerry Hicks, *Ask And It Is Given* (Hay House, 2004).

4. Eg. See Rupert Sheldrake, *A New Science Of Life* (Blond and Briggs, 1981).

5. Eg. See Fritjof Capra, *The Turning Point* (Simon & Schuster, 1982), Marilyn Ferguson, *The Aquarian Conspiracy* (Paladin, 1982), Gary Zukav, *The Seat Of The Soul* (Simon & Schuster, 1990), Amit Goswami, *The Self-Aware Universe* (Tarcher/ Putnam, 1995), Lynn McTaggart, *The Field* (Element, 2003) or almost any of the thousands of books on my own shelves!

6. Neale Donald Walsch, *What God Wants* (Hodder & Stoughton, 2005).

7. Eg. See the writings of Neil Douglas-Klotz for translations and interpretations of Jesus' teachings from the original Aramaic – which give a very different picture from traditional Christianity. Jesus probably taught at many different levels, but seemed to offer a holistic, empowering and mystical viewpoint that was based on unconditional love.

8. From 'A Great Wagon' by Rumi. Eg. See Coleman Barks with John Moyne (transl.), *The Essential Rumi* (Penguin, 1995), p.36.

9. Eg. See Matthew Fox, *Original Blessing* (Bear & Co, 1983).

CHAPTER TWO: THE WONDROUS SECRET

10. Jane Roberts, *The Nature of Personal Reality: A Seth Book* (Prentice Hall, 1974), p.23.

11. Eg. Amit Goswami, *The Self-Aware Universe* (Tarcher/Putnam, 1995).

CHAPTER THREE: FEEL YOUR WAY INTO THE FLOW

12. Candace Pert, *Molecules of Emotion* (Simon & Schuster, 1998), p.265.

13. The teachings of Abraham focus largely on our emotional guidance. See www.abraham-hicks.com, or Esther and Jerry Hicks, *Ask And It Is Given* (Hay House, 2004). See also my own book *Wild Love* (Piatkus, 2006) and books on energy psychology such as *The Healing Power of EFT and Energy Psychology* by David Feinstein, Donna Eden and Gary Craig (Piatkus, 2006).

14. Candace Pert, *Molecules of Emotion* (Simon & Schuster, 1998).

15. This is a much-used metaphor in the teachings of Abraham. See www.abraham-hicks.com, or Esther and Jerry Hicks, *Ask And It Is Given* (Hay House, 2004).

CHAPTER FOUR: THE INNER VOICE OF LOVE

16. Paul Ferrini, *Love Without Conditions* (Heartways, 1994/2003), p.127.

17. Eugene Trivizas and Helen Oxenbury, *The Three Little Wolves And The Big Bad Pig* (Egmont, 1995).

18. Bruce Lipton, *The Biology of Belief* (Cygnus Books, 2005).

19. Feeling 'bound by loyalty' is characteristic of living in fear-mode. It means you are being ruled by fear, habit and insecurity,

rather than reaching towards your higher self. See Stephanie Mines' book below – or books on co-dependency such as Melody Beattie, *Codependent No More* (Hazelden, 1987).

20. See Stephanie Mines, *We Are All In Shock* (Career Press, 2003) for more on how and why we flip into fear-mode – and a practical method of healing based on gentle touch known as the TARA approach. Energy psychology, such as EFT or TAT, is also excellent for releasing shock and trauma from the energy system – and thus getting back into the flow. eg. See www.emofree.com or www.tatlife.com, and my earlier book *Wild Love* (Piatkus, 2006).

21. Marshall Rosenberg's method of non-violent communication (NVC) offers tools for healthy communication and conflict resolution. See www.cnvc.org or Marshall B Rosenberg, *Nonviolent Communication* (PuddleDancer, 2003).

22. Marianne Williamson, *Enchanted Love* (Touchstone, 2001).

23. See my earlier book, *Wild Love* (Piatkus, 2006) for more on patterns of relating, and why we need unconditional love for healthy intimate relationships. I also recommend Jett Psaris and Marlena S Lyons, *Undefended Love* (New Harbinger, 2000) as a model for discovering the kind of love and intimacy that sets you free to be who you are, rather than splitting your energy and maintaining your defences.

24. Paulo Coelho, *The Zahir* (HarperCollins, 2006).

25. I discuss this control-sacrifice pattern in more detail in my earlier book *Wild Love* (Piatkus, 2006).

CHAPTER FIVE: BECOMING A LASER BEAM

26. Sanaya Roman, *Personal Power Through Awareness* (H J Kramer, 1986), p.2.

27. William Tiller, *Science and Human Transformation* (Pavior, 1997), p.196.

28. Bruce Lipton, *The Biology of Belief* (Cygnus Books, 2005). Dawson Church, *The Genie in Your Genes* (Elite Books, 2007).

29. Eg. See books by Deepak Chopra, Bernie S Siegel, Larry Dossey, Rudolph Ballentine, Bruce Lipton, Caroline Myss,

Norman Shealy, Donna Eden and countless other pioneers of the new medicine.

30. Deepak Chopra, *Unconditional Life* (Bantam, 1991), pp.44–5.

31. From the teachings of Abraham. See www.abraham-hicks. com, or Esther and Jerry Hicks, *Ask And It Is Given* (Hay House, 2004).

CHAPTER SIX: LIGHTEN UP AND LET GO

32. Deepak Chopra, *The Way of the Wizard* (Rider, 1996), p.123.

33. Joseph Campbell with Bill Moyers, *The Power of Myth* (Doubleday & Co, 1988), p.120.

CHAPTER SEVEN: EVERYTHING IS UNFOLDING PERFECTLY

34. John F Demartini, *Count Your Blessings* (Element, 2003), p.84.

35. This perspective on the role of contrast came largely from the teachings of Abraham. See www.abraham-hicks.com, or Esther and Jerry Hicks, *Ask And It Is Given* (Hay House, 2004) and other books.

36. The story is told in my earlier book *Wild Love* (Piatkus, 2006).

37. From 'You Darkness', in *Selected Poems of Rainer Maria Rilke*, translated by Robert Bly (HarperPerennial, 1981).

38. John O'Donohue, *Eternal Echoes* (Bantam, 1998), p.231.

CHAPTER EIGHT: YOU *CAN* MAKE A DIFFERENCE

39. Marianne Williamson, *A Return To Love* (Aquarian, 1992), p.161.

40. This is a sub-personality that I call the Responsible Parent, or Hero-Rescuer. See note below. For an excellent approach to working with sub-personalities, see Hal Stone and Sidra L. Stone, *Embracing Our Selves* (New World Library, 1989) and *Partnering* (New World Library, 2000). I see a sub-personality as a collective of habitual thoughts or vibrations.

41. Hal and Sidra Stone would probably call this voice The

Pusher. For the sake of simplicity, I lump all the controlling, critical parental ego-selves together under the term the
Controller-Judge. The complementary self which meekly gives
in to its demands, feels guilty and sacrifices itself, is what I
call the Tame Child. These two ego-selves account for many
of the dysfunctional patterns in relationships, as well as within
our own psyches. Another problematic self is the Responsible
Parent, which tends to feel responsible for others' happiness and
well-being – and often disempowers, protects or rescues others.
Many of the dramas in everyday life involve these three ego-
selves – also known as the Persecutor, Victim and Hero-Rescuer
– which together create 'drama triangles'.

CHAPTER NINE: DARE TO LIVE, DARE TO DREAM
42. Pat Rodegast and Judith Stanton, *Emmanuel's Book III*
(Bantam, 1994), p.46.
43. From 'The Summer Day' by Mary Oliver, *New and Selected
Poems* (Beacon Press, 1992), p.94.
44. For inspiration, try Steve Davey, *Unforgettable Places To See
Before You Die* (BBC, 2004) or Steve Watkins and Clare Jones,
Unforgettable Things To Do Before You Die (BBC, 2005).

AFTERWORD
45. When Moses went to Mount Sinai, he was apparently
enraged with the state of his nation – and when you hear the
voice of God/Source from rage it may sound judgmental and
righteous. (That is, slightly higher on the emotional ladder.)
From a state of unconditional love and joy, the voice of God
sounds very different.

I have often sensed that, in a past life, I became a young
female disciple of Jesus soon after the crucifixion (and that
there were many women disciples, though they were omitted
from The Bible). My hunch is that *Life is a Gift*, and the Ten
Invitations, mark a culmination of the work I began in that
lifetime.

Index

Note: entries in **bold** refer to exercises